THE MOST INCREDIBLE BOXING STORIES EVER TOLD

INSPIRATIONAL AND LEGENDARY TALES FROM THE GREATEST BOXERS OF ALL TIME

Hank Patton

TABLE OF CONTENTS

ATTENTION:

DO YOU WANT MY FUTURE BOOKS AT HEAVY DISCOUNTS AND EVEN FOR FREE?

HEAD OVER TO WWW.SECRETREADS.COM AND JOIN MY SECRET BOOK CLUB!

INTRODUCTION

Boxing is a dangerous sport. Even calling it a sport is a misnomer. You play sports like you play baseball or basketball. You don't *play* boxing. There's nothing "play" about it. Boxing is raw and brutal. That's what makes it so captivating to watch.

The primal nature of boxing makes it universally understood. Almost every culture participates in boxing. The ones that don't participate, still understand the rules: hit the other person and avoid getting hit. You can't explain any other sport with such simplicity.

The physicality of boxing often undermines the intellect. Combatants have to outwit as much as they need to outpunch the opponent. Throughout boxing's history, there are ample cases where the "Davids" have dominated the "Goliaths" through strategy and skill over strength and aggression.

Matches become wars of attrition - the art of managing energy, injury, strength, and the scorecard. Boxers that fail to conserve don't survive late rounds. Successful boxers understand when to preserve and when to unleash to tip the scales in their favor. This is at the core of boxing: finding weaknesses and exploiting them.

This book contains 15 of boxing's most incredible and significant narratives. Between these pages, you'll find boxing stories about comebacks, upsets, and, of course, stunning knockouts. Some stories even transcend boxing, dipping into the realms of civil rights or world affairs.

Whether you're a fighter, a fan, or both, understanding boxing's history is important. The knowledge serves you inside the ring and out. You'll learn new things about the most recognizable names in boxing. Plus, you may even pick up a new strategy or two!

CHAPTER 1:

RACISM IN THE RING: JEFFERIES VERSUS JOHNSON

Tommy Burns isn't a name many boxing fans recall, which is fair considering his career occurred a century ago. Yet, he has an impressive resume. He is the only heavyweight boxing champion of the world to hail from Canada. He is also the first *World* Champion, defending his title in various countries across multiple continents. He fought in Ireland, France, America, Australia, England, and beyond.

Most of all, boxing history recalls Tommy Burns as the first boxer to give an African-American a shot at the heavyweight title. "I will defend my title against all comers, none barred," he once said. "By this, I mean white, black, Mexican, Indian, or any other nationality. I propose to be the champion of the world, not the white, or the Canadian, or the American."

Burns took the title of World Champion seriously.

True to his word, he accepted a fight with Jack Johnson; the first heavyweight championship match to include a Black contender. The bout was held in Sydney, Australia. Johnson had an obvious size advantage over Burns. The challenger weighed 24 pounds more than the defending champion and had a few more inches too. This was not unfamiliar territory for Burns; he was typically the smaller contender in the ring.

The Sydney match was arranged for 20 rounds, each lasting the standard three minutes. The fight was stopped in Round 14. Burns was badly hurt, his face swollen and puffy, and he couldn't muster up a counter-offense to Johnson's punching. Burns made no excuse for his loss, stating that Johnson was one of the best he had ever faced.

The rest of the world, particularly America, was not so willing to accept Johnson's win or his status as the champion of the world. Almost immediately, there was an effort to find a White challenger to usurp Johnson and reclaim the title.

Black and White

It was the height of Jim Crowism. Slavery was close enough in the past that people still remembered it. Only months before Johnson's title win, a mob of around 5,000 Whites in Springfield, Illinois - President Lincoln's political home state - had attacked African Americans in the streets, burned Black-owned businesses, and destroyed homes.

Few of the White rioters faced any serious charges beyond rioting, malicious mischief, and destruction of property. The Black citizens involved, many of whom only tried to defend their lives and property, were indicted for assault with intent to murder, assault with a deadly weapon, and worse. It showed that race was still a significant and volatile issue even in the post-slavery era, in a place largely considered to be accepting of African-Americans.

So, imagine the disdain of White Americans when they learned the new heavyweight champion of the world was a Black man. It sent a message that the greatest boxer, the toughest man in the world, was Black. This was exactly what James Jeffries felt he needed to correct when he challenged Johnson in 1910. "I am going into this fight for the sole purpose of proving that a white man is better than a negro."

James J. Jeffries was a remarkable heavyweight champion. He was undefeated in over 22 fights, including several defenses of the world heavyweight title, the same title that Jack Johnson now held. After defeating Jack Munroe with an early knockout, Jeffries retired in May 1905. He hadn't boxed in six years but was everyone's first pick to reclaim the crown and restore boxing's prestige. He became, as writer Jack London noted, the "Great White Hope."

Putting race aside, Jeffries had another motivation to take on the fight with Johnson - money. Tex Rickard, the fight's promoter, understood the fight's significance and the draw that it would bring. Not only were you pitting the old and undefeated champion against the new title holder, but it would certainly attract huge crowds of Whites and Blacks.

Richard was so confident in the fight's massive revenue that, on top of a guaranteed purse of $40,000, he gave Jeffries a personal contract for $75,000. The $115,000 that Jeffries would earn from the fight, no matter the outcome, is equivalent to approximately $3.5M today - not a bad reason to pause your retirement.

There was one problem with the former champion's unplanned return to boxing. Since retiring in 1905, Jeffries had been relaxing and enjoying life, which meant he was in a completely different shape than his boxing days. Now weighing over 300 pounds, the former champion needed to lose over 100 pounds in very little time. Johnson, meanwhile, was already in peak fighting condition.

Jeffries' size and out-of-shape physique were a chief concern to fans that were touting him as their great hope to "restore boxing's glory" (in other words, remove the African-American title holder). The concerns grew when Jeffries was rarely seen in the short window leading up to the fight.

Miraculously, when he finally appeared again, he had lost over 100 pounds and was in peak condition. Around 1,000 spectators watched the chiseled Jeffries spar with Joe Choynski. Choynski was an interesting bridge between Jeffries and Johnson. He was one of only two boxers to go the distance with Jeffries and walk away with a draw. Choynski had also won a victory by knockout against Johnson in 1901. Jeffries hoped to pick Choynski's brain to gain insight into a winning strategy against his future opponent.

Even with Jeffries coming back in incredible shape, many felt it wouldn't be enough. Johnson was a physical specimen. After viewing both fighters, John L. Sullivan, a former champion himself, said that Johnson would only lose if he lacked skill on the day of the fight.

The Fight of the Century

On the day of the fight, dubbed "The Fight of the Century" for its cultural significance and the reputations of each boxer, trains poured into Reno, Nevada, unloading hordes of people looking to catch the fight. Those with deep pockets would be fortunate enough to purchase ringside tickets for $50 (around $1,500 today). Those without money for admittance would try to climb the walls and barriers of the recently-constructed arena.

Aside from the throngs of spectators, the other unavoidable characteristic of the match's setting was the temperature. Thermometers at the time of the fight read 110 degrees Fahrenheit. With the match set for 45 rounds, both boxers would have to manage the heat on top of whatever their opponent threw at them.

The fight started slowly, whether because of the heat or just a matter of both fighters feeling one another out. Jeffries had initially said he would try to end the fight as quickly as possible. Perhaps, the heat slowed the older boxer.

Conversely, Johnson preferred to start slowly; wearing boxers down and then capitalizing in later rounds was his strategy.

Spectators in Round 1 also witnessed Johnston employ a special strategy specific to this fight. He had told the press he would beat Jeffries in the clinch, taking away his opponent's ability to throw inside power punches. He planned to hold Jeffries in such a way that he'd pin his arms back. While the 1st round was slow, Johnson's tactic seemed to work to neutralize the former champion.

The slow pace continued for the 2nd and 3rd rounds. The boxers continued to feel each other out and only occasionally land punches. The tempo changed in Round 4. Johnson challenged Jeffries with multiple punches. True to his proposed strategy, he kept Jeffries arms back before stinging him with an overhand or uppercut punch.

As the rounds progressed, Johnson's strategy shone as superior. In the heat of the Nevada summer sun and the stinging punches from the champion, James J. Jeffries was fading quickly. The more time that passed in the match, the more opportunities Johnson found to pummel his opponent and successfully defend his title.

Jeffries was able to withstand the punishment until the 15th round. By then, the sun was even getting to the younger Johnson.

After the fight, Johnson would state that he knew the fight was over during the pace-changing 4th round. After hitting Jeffries with a stiff uppercut, the reigning champion saw a telling look in his opponent's eyes. In his own words, "the old ship was sinking."

Jeffries was humble in defeat. While critics of the fight, predominantly White, were ready with a slew of excuses for the once-undefeated fighter (age, heat, early stoppage to the fight - you name it), Jeffries didn't mince his words. "I could never have whipped Johnson at my best. I couldn't have hit him. No, I couldn't have reached him in 1,000 years," he stated.

These words quickly put a stop to the critics. No one could again claim that Johnson's title was hollow. Or that he hadn't beaten a *real* champion. Jack Johnson won fairly over James J. Jeffries. He won with such overwhelming certainty that there was no explanation other than him being the superior boxer.

Riots

Preceding the fight, *The New York Times* published an editorial regarding the fight. The "enlightened" author had this to say about the meeting between Jeffries and Johnson:

> *"If the black man wins, thousands and thousands of his ignorant brothers will misinterpret his victory as*

justifying claims to much more than mere physical equality with their white neighbors."

These sentiments, or those similar and equally misguided, echoed in the heads of Whites nationwide. By the evening after the fight, the evening of July 4, tensions boiled over. On America's Independence Day, nationalism and patriotism were supposed to be at an all-time high. Yet, many people felt defeated as the heavyweight champion was still an African-American man. Unfortunately, 1910 was a time when patriotism was primarily if not exclusively, a leisure of White Americans.

Across the country, Whites were unhappy, embarrassed, and mad; their "Great White Hope" had been defeated. Nearby, their Black neighbors were in the highest of spirits. They had just watched their champion - the champion of the world - defeat that same "Great White Hope." It was more than a boxing match; it was seen as a victory for the Black race.

The jubilation of Blacks and the scorn of Whites quickly collided in the streets and neighborhoods across America. In total, there were riots in 25 states, stretching to every corner of the country. Fifty major cities saw dangerous activity from Whites and Blacks. In total, between 15 and 26 people died in the riots (the numbers vary between sources). Hundreds were injured. The majority of casualties were Blacks.

In Houston, Texas, Charles Williams, a Black supporter of Johnson, was cut across his neck for publicly cheering for the champion's victory over Jeffries. In Norfolk, Virginia, 300 members of the US Navy, all White, roamed the streets looking for Black people that might be celebrating the outcome of the boxing match.

In Wheeling, West Virginia, a Black man driving a car deemed too expensive for him by a White mob was stopped and hung. Black partygoers in Pittsburgh, PA were besieged by police for blocking traffic and harassing the public.

Inhabitants of New York City saw anywhere up to 11 different riots, most originating from White mobs entering Black neighborhoods and setting fire to homes and businesses. There were untold injuries and a few deaths from these violent activities.

You could practically throw a dart at a map of the United States and find a riot-related story at the projectile's landing point.

In response to the nationwide destruction, it became illegal to transport boxing films across state lines. Additionally, many states banned the showing or possession of the *Jeffries-Johnson World's Championship Boxing Contest*, a two-hour film of the match. Later, President Roosevelt issued another ban, outlawing prizefighting altogether. He stated that gambling, match-fixing, and other unscrupulous activities had infected the sport.

Roosevelt's rhetoric during this declaration was crafty. By addressing the crookedness of boxing, Roosevelt subtly gave angered Whites a scapegoat for their humiliation behind Jeffries' loss without casting blame on any African Americans. It wasn't anyone's fault but the unscrupulous fixers lurking in the shadows of the boxing community.

The casualty, caught in the crossfire of precarious race relations, was boxing itself. With prizefighting outlawed across the country, professional boxing had few bastions left to host fights. And, with the crown of heavyweight champion of the world still resting on the head of an African-American, White audiences tuned out, preferring to ignore the sport entirely rather than give the champion any attention or merit. At least until they could find a new "White Hope."

Did You Know?

- Another interesting fact about Tommy Burns comes from his trilogy with Australian boxer Bill Squires. The three met in the ring in America, Europe, and Australia, becoming the only time in history that two boxers fought for the title across three continents.

- Jack Johnson may have grown up in the South, but he didn't experience racism during his childhood. Galveston, Texas was inhabited by poor Whites and Blacks. Both races shared in the struggles and had no time or need to propose superiority over one another.

- In recent times, an internet post circulated claiming Jack Johnson invented the monkey wrench. Johnson did receive a patent for *improvements* to the tool but did not invent the wrench himself.

- Jeffries Avenue in Burbank, California, is named after Jim Jeffries. The boxer lived in Burbank for much of his life and died there. There is also a plaque in his honor that is now in the Gordon R. Howard Museum in Burbank.

- While Jeffries adopted the nickname "The Great White Hope" for the Johnson fight, his less-offensive nickname was "The Boilermaker." It was his first profession before a career in boxing.

- Tex Rickard, the fight's promoter, tried to entice President Taft to referee the match. When Taft declined, Rickard asked Sir Arthur Conan Doyle, author of *The Adventures of Sherlock Holmes*. Doyle also declined. Rickard then decided to referee himself.

CHAPTER 2:

JACK DEMPSEY TOPPLES THE POTTAWATOMIE GIANT

In 1910, a boxing promoter was traveling through Kansas when he spotted massive hay bales moving unnaturally on the horizon. He slowed to investigate further and saw a colossal figure tossing the 500-pound bales as if they were pillows. The man was Jess Willard.

The six-foot-six, 225-pound giant became an immediate success in the boxing world. He dominated through sheer size and force. How much force did Willard pack behind his punches? Well, in his fifth organized fight, he hit a young and promising fighter named John "Bull" Young hard enough to drive a piece of jawbone into the boxer's brain during the 9th round.

Young collapsed and died from the massive hit, resulting in Willard facing second-degree murder after the fight. Defense attorney Earl Rogers successfully repelled the charges, allowing Willard to continue his boxing career. Notably, Rogers was a legendary defense attorney that protected clients from murder charges 74 out of 77 times.

Free from killing a man in the ring, Willard continued pushing through the heavyweight boxing ranks as easily as he had tossed hay bales in Kansas. At a time when Black and White Americans were separate but far from equal, Willard became a fan favorite for defeating Jack Johnson in a 26-round fight in Cuba. The contest brought the title of heavyweight champion back to White America.

In present times, it's hard to see this feat as a positive. However, in 1915, Willard taking the title back revitalized boxing. It was an unfortunate time in American history when Whites dominated every facet of life. Willard claiming the title from Johnson restored the "purity" of boxing in the minds of White Americans of the time.

With Jack Johnson out of the picture, boxing could institute the same unspoken Whites-only rules that baseball and other sports used to keep Blacks from competing. This also ensured Willard's superiority in boxing by limiting his potential competitors. That was until, four years after Willard defeated Johnson, a new fighter challenged him: Jack Dempsey.

Kid Blackie

Jack Dempsey's story is a classic American rags-to-riches tale. Born William Harrison Dempsey, his father Hiram moved the family around often to pursue work around the San Luis Valley and Colorado River Delta areas. Dempsey sometimes accompanied his father and his older brothers to work to perform odd jobs.

Later, the family moved to Montrose. The construction of the Gunnison Tunnel promised steady work for the Dempsey family. Hiram and the older Dempsey boys quickly found jobs on the project. Celia, Dempsey's mother, even opened a successful restaurant serving tunnel workers. Jack Dempsey helped his mother, washing dishes and serving tables.

While it seemed like an idyllic setting for the family, they moved once more to Provo, Utah. This time, it was the young Jack Dempsey who didn't stay in town long. Shortly after turning 16, the future boxing star left home. With little money to his name, he hopped freight trains, heading back east to Montrose.

Aside from finding short-term work in various mines and construction sites, Dempsey's primary source of income became barfights at local saloons. "I can't sing, and I can't dance, but I can lick any SOB in the house," was Dempsey's invitation to bar patrons, according to the future champion's autobiography.

Had this challenge come from Jack Dempsey, the heavyweight champion, people would have been less inclined to participate. However, Dempsey, at this time, wasn't even an adult. He hadn't even adopted the name Jack yet. He was thin and carried a boyish voice late into puberty, which made his provocation all the more comical and enticing to miners, bar patrons, and anyone else within earshot.

The laughter and jeers from the crowd quickly subsided once the fighting began. Despite his size and high-pitched voice, Dempsey rarely lost. Sometimes, he'd pick up small winnings from those betting. Mostly, he fought to get a hot meal and a room for the night in return for the "entertainment" he provided.

Through these fights, Dempsey gained a reputation under his fighting name, "Kid Blackie." It's unclear how this name got started. Was it Dempsey's creation or simply how spectators referred to the young kid with a mop of dark, black hair? It may have also been due to the abundance of black eyes he left behind in the small mining towns he visited.

By the time Dempsey arrived in Montrose, it's estimated he had participated in over 400 fights. Boxing was no longer a means to pick up extra money but a career path. In Montrose, he met boxers, Charley Diehl and Fred Woods. Diehl gave him his first pair of boxing gloves and began giving him some proper training. The trio even planned and executed a local fighting exhibition between Wood and Dempsey, with the latter winning.

After finishing his first professional fight, Dempsey traveled across Colorado to pursue more organized matches. Eventually, he met manager Jack Kearns, moved to California, and took his career and training to new levels.

Under Kearns, Dempsey's reputation soared, particularly after winning 12 fights in a row, including several consecutive first-round knockouts. As the newest talk of the boxing community, the next step became apparent:

challenge the heavyweight champion of the world, Jess Willard.

Toledo, Ohio; July 4, 1919

Toledo may seem like an odd choice to host a boxing title fight. At the time, it didn't even have a large enough stadium to hold the thousands of boxing fans about to descend on the city. Tex Rickard, the fight's promoter, had to have a temporary one built for this occasion, then torn down after. Toledo hosted the event only because it could; it was one of the few places in the country to still allow prizefighting boxing matches.

The buzz surrounding the fight between Jack Dempsey and Jess Willard was one-sided. Willard now weighed over 240 pounds and was almost a half-foot taller. Dempsey, the up-and-comer, didn't have the typical muscle-bound physique of a heavyweight contender. He was scrawny and wiry, weighing only 187 pounds.

Having already killed a man in the ring once, Willard said, "This will be one of the easiest bouts I've ever had," and requested to be indemnified and legally protected should he do the same to Dempsey in the ring. This was a fear many sportswriters and boxing professionals held, especially given the size disparity between the two fighters.

However, this was Jack Dempsey, a young fighter who, for years now, had built a living and a legacy on boxing fighters much bigger than him. He was undeterred by Willard's size or history. If anyone had the skill to topple the Pottawatomie Giant, it was Dempsey.

The perceptions of fans and boxing professionals quickly changed in the first minute of the fight. Those worried about Dempsey's well-being against the much larger Willard flipped. The unstoppable giant was in noticeably grave trouble. Hidden by Dempsey's scrawny build were iron-like punches and intense ferocity.

Opponents would say that hitting Dempsey felt like punching an oak tree. Over the years, he had toughened his skin using beef brine and horse urine. According to one individual's report, when he hit back, it was like a building fell on you. And Dempsey didn't hit you just once. To the untrained eye, he seemed to attack like a wild dog. Yet, there was a precision to his assault that relied on years of training and experience.

It was this level of accurate beating that he dispensed on Willard. Dempsey adeptly dodged his large opponent's attempts to keep him at bay, finding opportunities to get inside the long reach. Close to Willard's body, Dempsey could unleash a flurry of punches. When Kid Blackie connected with a left hook, he dropped Willard to the floor.

It was the first time an opponent had knocked down the giant, but it wouldn't be the last time in this fight.

Willard looked momentarily dazed from the punch, but he got up quickly. A few seconds later, Dempsey connected again and dropped Big Jess a second time. Again, Willard rose, and again, Dempsey sat him back down. During the 1st round, Willard would go down seven times. The damage beneath the surface was even more troubling.

The extent of Willard's injuries varies across various reports and retellings throughout history. The most common details, if accurate, are that Dempsey's first knockdown punch broke Willard's jaw in more than 10 places. Subsequent Dempsey punches knocked out as many as six teeth. Willard also suffered from damaged ribs, a cracked cheekbone, and more. It was a miracle the fight lasted through three rounds; Willard could not get out of his corner at the start of the fourth. His resolve to last as long as he did is considered one of the most courageous acts in boxing's history.

Willard's courage aside, Jack Dempsey was the new heavyweight champion.

Controversy

Any fight on the scale of the Dempsey and Willard bout is bound to have some controversy. Nowadays, social media gives us all the dirt the next day - or sometimes only minutes after the fight ends. In 1919, fighting controversies didn't pop up until years later, usually at a time when the fight was only a memory and the details had grown fuzzy for everyone.

Immediately following the fight, Willard remarked:

> *"Dempsey is a remarkable hitter. It was the first time that I had ever been knocked off my feet. I have sent many birds home in the same bruised condition that I am in, and now I know how they felt. I sincerely wish Dempsey all the luck possible and hope that he garnishes all the riches that come with the championship."*

He changed his tune later on, claiming that he lost to "gangsterism." In other words, Willard boldly claimed the fight was fixed. This was a perpetual fear of the times. The Willard-Dempsey fight happened the same year that fixers managed to rig baseball's World Series. Baseball was seen as a more legitimate and organized sport than boxing. When the 1919 World Series fix came to light, every game, match, tournament, and championship came under question across all sports and betting events.

A central part of the fixing theory is the inconsistent reports surrounding Willard's injuries. Despite all the reports that Dempsey had, for brevity's sake, broken Willard's face and body, other sources claimed the former champion had few injuries. The *New York Times* noted swelling in Willard's face during the fight but no serious injuries. Similarly, the *Topeka Daily Capital* published an interview with Willard less than two weeks after the fight, stating, "The ex-champion didn't have any black eye, nor any signs that he was injured in any way."

Willard ignited another controversy later in his life. During a 1960 interview with *BBC Sport,* he claimed Dempsey held a metal bolt on the outside of his glove, which he used to slash and cut Willard's face. The ex-champion even produced the metal object from a small box, saying it was found on the floor after the fight. Supporters of the theory even suggest the grainy footage of the fight shows something falling onto the mat near Dempsey before someone in the corner grabs it.

This theory aligned with other claims that Dempsey loaded his gloves with plaster of Paris, a fast-acting, cement-like substance. Jack Kearns, Dempsey's manager, brought this controversy to light after the two had a falling out. He came to *Sports Illustrated* with a tale that he had bet $10,000 on Dempsey to record a first-round knockout. To secure his winnings, he applied plaster of Paris to the fighter's wrappings.

Both the loaded glove and the hidden metal object have been largely debunked. Not only are Dempsey's hands in clear view of everyone before the fight, but Willard even examines them. Eyewitness accounts further debunk the plaster of Paris concept, saying Kearns never had any contact with Dempsey's wrappings.

The hidden object theory is also proven incorrect by the fight's footage. There are several instances where the two fighters clinch or Dempsey holds onto the ropes. Neither would have been possible if the fighter was clutching any object. It would appear that - if Willard felt he was being hit by cement or hidden objects - it was only because Dempsey's punches felt like being hit that hard.

Dempsey's Legacy

The reality was Jack Dempsey was a superb boxer. He exposed Willard as a giant fighter but not a sound boxer. Dempsey had skill and technique that more than made up for the physical size difference between the two men. And, if there were any doubts about the legitimacy of Dempsey's win, one needed only to wait for the rest of his career to unfold.

He successfully defended his heavyweight champion honors, winning most of the time by knockout punches and sometimes as early as the 2nd round. He ultimately lost the title to Gene Tunney, and his career ended shortly after. Nonetheless, he had established himself as a legend in the boxing world and an icon among the American people. His celebrity status was on a similar level to that of Babe Ruth, Charles Lindbergh, Charlie Chaplin, and others.

Dempsey would continue to participate in boxing events, although not professional ones. In under two years, he estimated that he took part in close to 100 boxing exhibition matches. His fights, both professional and not, drew the most substantial crowds the boxing world had ever seen. With stakes in the fights' attendance revenue, Dempsey quickly became as rich as he was successful. He used most of his wealth to open businesses and help friends, furthering his legacy as one of the most liked human beings alive in the 1920s and 1930s.

When the International Boxing Hall of Fame opened in 1990, taking up the torch from *The Ring* magazine's Boxing Hall of Fame (disbanded in 1987), Dempsey was a member of the inaugural class, along with names like Muhammad Ali, Joe Frazier, Joe Louis, Gene Tunney, Jack Johnson, and others. Willard would not be inducted until 2003.

Did You Know?

- Willard turned his celebrity status as a boxer into other entertainment ventures. He was in a vaudeville show and appeared in two feature films: *The Challenge of Chance* and *The Prizefighter and the Lady*.

- Jack Dempsey also appeared in *The Prizefighter and the Lady*, playing the role of a boxing promoter.

- Willard had the longest life of a heavyweight champion, dying at age 86. His record was passed by Dempsey, who died at age 87.

- Several times throughout his career, Jack Dempsey participated in fights that drew millions of dollars from attendees. These seven-figure matches were record-breaking at the time.

- When Willard took the title from Jack Johnson, the fight lasted a remarkable 26 rounds. It's a wonder either fighter could leave the ring on their own accord.

- When Willard could not return to the fight with Dempsey between the 3rd and 4th rounds, he became the first champion to give up the title from the corner stool.

CHAPTER 3:

MIKE TYSON, EVANDER HOLYFIELD, AND "THE BITE"

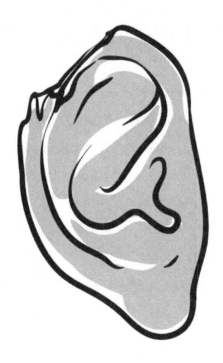

Mike Tyson is one of those celebrities and sports figures known worldwide, like Snoop Dogg, Shaquille O'Neil, and David Beckham. You could put him in any city in the world, and the inhabitants would recognize him. There are a few reasons behind Tyson's larger-than-life reputation.

The first is, of course, his boxing record. In 58 total fights, Tyson won 50 times, including 44 through knockout. He has six career losses and two no-decisions. More impressive was the beginning of Tyson's boxing career. He wouldn't experience a loss until his 38th career fight. These legendary numbers put Tyson in the ring with names like Muhammad Ali (56 wins and five losses).

It wasn't just Tyson's record that brought attention to his name; it was *how* he would dispatch his opponents. His first 19 fights were all victories by knockout, many in the 1st round. Tyson's fierce fighting style and tremendous punching power were reminiscent of Jack Dempsey and helped give the boxer fearsome nicknames like Kid Dynamite and Iron Mike.

Another reason for Tyson's worldwide fame is his acting career. Tyson has appeared in several movies and TV shows, typically playing himself. His acting resume includes titles like *How I Met Your Mother, The Hangover, Law & Order, Entourage, Rocky Balboa,* and many others.

The final case for Tyson's reputation is not a favorable one. He led a life outside the ring that produced a slew of controversies and negative press. He even served time in prison on rape charges. Combine this with messy divorces, firing managers and trainers, and other drama in the fighter's personal life, and you have someone who rarely left the public eye in the late 80s and 90s. As much as he was a persistent producer of knockouts, he also made tabloid headlines at an equally impressive rate.

Arguably, the most notable paper-selling headline came from his rematch fight with Evander Holyfield on June 28, 1997. Tyson's actions in that fight didn't just make the news; they put an unfortunate and permanent blemish on his boxing career.

Buster Douglas

Before diving into the fights between Holyfield and Tyson, it's critical to first talk about Buster Douglas. Douglas was the bridge between these two fighters, holding the title of undisputed heavyweight champion for eight months. By defeating Mike Tyson in Japan on February 11, 1990, Douglas claimed the World Boxing Council, World Boxing Association, and International Boxing Federation titles. Douglas then relinquished the authority to Evander Holyfield 256 days later.

The fight between Tyson and Buster Douglas may be the most remarkable upset in boxing history. After all, you have an undefeated and seemingly unstoppable Tyson versus a fighter with mixed success. Douglas ranked seventh in *Ring Magazine's* list of the best heavyweight boxers of the time.

There was so little faith in the challenger that most betting institutes refused to post odds on the fight. The Mirage casino was the exception, giving odds 42/1 in favor of Tyson. The press responsible for covering the fight had similar confidence. When Japanese customs agents asked Ed Schuyler of the Associated Press how long he'd be working in the country, he answered, "About ninety seconds." This was the perception that many boxing analysts shared: the fight was going to be yet another quick and dominant win for Tyson.

Iron Mike's corner also didn't give Douglas much hope. There was little preparation for the bout, short-sightedness that would prove critical during the fight. Tyson reportedly went to bed late the night before the fight, stating Douglas was an amateur he could beat even if he didn't sleep for weeks.

When the fight began, Douglas used his superior reach to keep Tyson at bay with a steady supply of jabs. This took away Tyson's most deadly weapon: his close-range punching power. At times when Tyson was able to find the inside angle, Douglas quickly evaded, clinched, or repelled Tyson with his punches. The repeated punishment from the contender's jab created swelling over Iron Mike's eye, making it harder and harder for him to see the oncoming punches.

The lack of preparation for the Douglas fight didn't just involve Tyson's lack of sleep. His corner also didn't have the typical ringside supplies. They didn't expect to need ice packs or an eye iron to prevent swelling. The best the heavyweight champion's corner could do was fill a rubber glove with ice water. It wasn't enough to fix the puffiness around the boxer's eye; Tyson was in danger, and there was seemingly no solution.

Douglas had put Tyson in a position he had yet to experience in his pro career. It was the first time the undefeated champion needed a come-from-behind win. The only glimmer of hope for Tyson came at the end of the 8th round; he landed a signature uppercut that put Douglas on his back. The challenger survived the count and the round but only barely.

At the start of the next frame, Tyson came out swinging, hoping Douglas was still hurting from the uppercut. Tyson's left eye was completely swollen shut by this point in the fight, making his offense inaccurate. By the close of the round, Douglas had Tyson backpedaling and against the ropes.

The fight was no longer a title defense for Tyson. It would be impossible for the reigning champion to secure a signature knockout with only one eye open. Douglas was simply too agile and knew his opponent was on the ropes, figuratively and physically. For Tyson, all that was left was to try to survive the final rounds.

In the 10th round, Tyson continued to push his offense, hoping for a lucky shot to drop his opponent and preserve his title. In an ironic twist, Douglas blasted Tyson with an uppercut, the same punch Tyson favored for his knockouts. The blow sent the champion's head back and stunned him completely. With his opponent defenseless, Douglas threw a series of punches when, for the first time, Iron Mike hit the canvas.

Tyson tried to get to his feet, struggling even to find his mouthguard on the floor of the ring. Ultimately, he couldn't beat referee Octavio Meyran's count. Buster Douglas was the new heavyweight champion. In press interviews after the fight, Douglas broke down in tears, stating he won because of his mother, Lula. She passed away just two weeks before the event, missing the opportunity to see her son achieve his dream of becoming a champion.

The winner's purse for Douglas' unbelievable victory over Tyson was $1.2M. On the other hand, despite losing, Tyson walked away with $6M.

A New Heavyweight Champion

There was some post-fight drama regarding the titles moving from Tyson to Douglas. At first, he only received the heavyweight IBF title. Tyson's team protested because they felt Douglas received a long count during the 8th-round knockdown. The WBA and WBC agreed and held the titles in limbo.

Eventually, Tyson's side withdrew their argument. This allowed all enterprises to recognize Douglas as the champion. Nonetheless, many fans of Iron Mike felt the outcome was unfair and urged for a rematch to happen. A second chapter in the Douglas-Tyson story never occurred because the heavyweight titles swiftly shifted to Evander Holyfield.

The same magazine that had posted Buster Douglas as the seventh-best heavyweight in the world had given the top honors to Evander Holyfield. Not only did he have an undefeated record, but Holyfield had already claimed the universal world cruiserweight champion title. After he became the champion in that weight class, he announced his transition into the heavyweight category.

After moving up in weight classes, Holyfield fought several notable opponents. First, he defeated James Tillis by a 5th-round knockout. Interestingly, Tillis was the first boxer to go the distance with Tyson, ending Iron Mike's streak of 19 wins by knockout. Next, he punished Pinklon Thomas, a former heavyweight champion, for seven rounds before trainer Angelo Dundee decided Thomas was unfit to return in the 8th round.

The following year, Holyfield started with a win over another former heavyweight champion, Michael Dokes. He went on to beat the Brazilian champion Adílson Rodrigues, then Alex Stewart, and, finally, Seamus McDonagh. He was the decisive pick among boxing fans to take on Tyson for the title. The Douglas upset spoiled those chances. Instead, Holyfield would have to take on the new champion to claim the titles.

The Holyfield-Douglas fight became a moment of truth for the defending champion. In the eyes of the boxing community, it would determine if Douglas' victory over Tyson was a fluke or not. A win against the undefeated Holyfield (24-0) would verify Douglas' status as a heavyweight champion.

Those with negative perceptions of Douglas quickly felt their views justified as the fight began. The defending champion was noticeably heavier than just a few months ago, having packed on about 15 pounds. In contrast, Holyfield weighed 38 pounds less. His smaller size kept him agile, allowing him to dominate Douglas for the first two rounds.

In the 3rd round, Douglas tried to throw a heavy uppercut. He was out of range, and the haymaker-style swing made it exceptionally easy for Holyfield to dodge. Now, Douglas was exposed, off-balance, and in trouble. The title challenger countered, shifting his weight to unload with a stiff, straight right. He would follow with a left uppercut, but Douglas was already falling to the canvas. He hit the ground and was frozen for the 10-count.

If Mike Tyson wanted to reclaim his undisputed heavyweight champion status, he would now have to go through Evander Holyfield.

Two Comebacks Converge

Evander Holyfield became the new champion at the end of 1990. Mike Tyson and Holyfield wouldn't meet for their first fight until 1996. By this time, Tyson had served his prison time for the rape of Desiree Washington. During his parole, he started a comeback tour in boxing.

His first return to the ring was an 89-second match against Peter McNeely. It was a victory by disqualification when McNeely's manager, trying to prevent further punishment, entered the ring after his fighter was knocked down for a second time. The fight set Pay Per View records, with over 1.5 million homes buying the fight. Despite the build-up surrounding the match, the quick knockout left many feeling that Tyson's team had given him a too-easy opponent for his return.

While Tyson certainly outclassed McNeely, it's hard to claim it was an intentionally easy fight based solely on the first-round decision. After all, this was Mike Tyson. He'd made a career on early knockouts. His next fights were all early-round knockouts. He beat Buster Mathis Jr. with a knockout in the 3rd round. A few months later, he recorded another third-round KO against Frank Bruno, securing the WBC title. He then added the WBA title from Bruce Seldon.

Holyfield was on a similar comeback tour. He was no longer the champion, having lost the title to Riddick Bowe. It was the first of a trilogy of fights and perhaps the most exciting of the three. Bowe was younger and stronger than Holyfield, outpunching him through most of the night. By comparison, Holyfield landed 39% of 161 punches. Bowe, on the other hand, found his mark 53% of the time, throwing almost 100 more punches than the champion.

The final rounds of the Holyfield-Bowe fight were particularly thrilling. In the 10th round, Howe looked like he was on the verge of knocking out Holyfield at any moment. Miraculously, the champion held on, even landing combinations of his own in the last seconds of the round. The 11th round also saw Bowe battering the defending champion, even knocking him down once. Still, Holyfield held on.

Behind on the scorecard, Holyfield's corner knew he needed a knockout to escape the fight with his title intact. He came out swinging in the final round, putting every remaining drop of energy into trying to put Howe down. Gassed and hurting from losing several rounds, Holyfield didn't have enough left in the tank to deliver. Bowe outlasted Holyfield's offense and took the heavyweight champion crown with a unanimous decision from the judges.

After a few more fights, including a rematch with Bowe, Holyfield went to a doctor for shoulder pain. He left diagnosed with a heart condition and promptly retired from boxing. A year later, Holyfield got a second opinion and passed an examination. It appeared his heart condition was a misdiagnosis.

Soon after returning to boxing, Holyfield and Tyson's comeback tours converged on November 9, 1996. The fight would decide the WBA heavyweight title, with Tyson defending the honors from Holyfield, the challenger.

A Rivalry

The match between Mike Tyson and Evander Holyfield was intense from the sound of the first bell. In their first meeting, Holyfield benefited from a clear strategic advantage. He had studied Tyson's fighting tendencies closely.

Thanks to his studying, he could anticipate when Tyson would throw his devastating left hook. Holyfield would quickly clinch and then, through impressive strength, push the 222-pound Tyson backwards. This made it impossible for Iron Mike to load his punches, while also giving Holyfield opportunities to throw punches as Tyson was backpedaling.

Holyfield's game plan worked perfectly. Aside from a hard punch at the beginning of the match and a strong combination in the 5th round, Tyson barely hurt Holyfield throughout the night. Even in the later rounds, Tyson couldn't adjust or find any openings against his opponent. Just like the Douglas fight, Iron Mike seemed unable to change his fate.

At the end of one round, Tyson threw a late punch, most likely out of frustration. Holyfield responded with a shot of his own. It was an early instance of the bad blood still to come between the two. The 6th round had another controversial moment between the two. Holyfield headbutted Tyson, cutting him. The act was deemed to be accidental by referee Mitch Halpern and the fight continued.

Holyfield delivered a left in the same round that put Tyson on his back. It was the first time since the Buster Douglas fight and only the second time in his career that an opponent had knocked Tyson down. The boxer got back to his feet, but Holyfield continued to pressure Iron Mike with his superior strategy.

There was a second headbutt incident in the 7th round. Both fighters came forward simultaneously; their heads met in the middle. Tyson was in audible pain and almost dropped, but again, the referee ruled the contact accidental. The incident, coupled with the beating Holyfield was dishing out, made it a challenge for Tyson to even survive the round. He repeatedly clinched the opponent to stay on his feet.

The next round was also about survival for Mike Tyson. Holyfield continued to use his strategy, making his opponent miss and countering with hard punches of his own. By the end of the 10th round, Tyson appeared to be on his last leg. Saved by the bell, Tyson came out in the next round, but Holyfield swiftly continued the onslaught. With Tyson backed against the ropes and barely able to stand, the official called the fight, giving Holyfield the victory by TKO.

In the aftermath of the fight, Tyson's side argued that Holyfield's headbutts were not accidental. The controversy damaged the legitimacy of the victory and Holyfield's possession of the WBA title. Again, fans of Tyson argued about the outcome, creating turmoil in the boxing community. Eight months later, the two boxers met for a rematch.

The Bite Fight

The Tyson-Holyfield rematch would go down in the annals of boxing history as one of the most notorious fights of all time. And, perhaps, one of the most unexpected and strange. Tensions were still high over the headbutting incidents in the first fight. Tyson and his management team continued to claim that Holyfield had won the previous battle unfairly, ignoring the referee's judgment that the head contact was accidental.

Initially, Mitch Halpern was named the referee. Tyson's team took issue with this, fearing that the same problems from the first match would happen again. They pleaded for a new referee for the rematch. The Nevada State Athletic Commission denied this request, creating a backlash from the Tyson team. Eventually, Halpern withdrew from the role on his own accord, citing that his presence as the third man would be a distraction. Mills Lane became the new referee.

The tensions surrounding Tyson and Holyfield nearly erupted in the 2nd round of the rematch. Holyfield ducked a heavy right from Tyson, but his head made contact with Tyson's in the process. Similar to the first fight, Holyfield's head produced a gash over Tyson's eye. Referee Mills Lane reviewed the tape and said the headbutt was unintentional, just like in the first fight. In the eyes of Tyson and his team, Holyfield had once again cheated and avoided any punishment. Tyson's frustration began to reach unstable levels.

At the start of the next round, Tyson tried to start without his mouthguard. The referee noticed and sent the fighter back to his corner to insert his mouthguard. It was a foreshadowing of what was to come. In the final minute of the 3rd round, Holyfield held Tyson in a clinch. The frustrated Tyson maneuvered his head to the side of Holyfield's and bit down on his ear.

Boxing fans saw the defending champion jump and shout in pain, holding his now-mangled ear. The bite would tear a small piece of cartilage from Holyfield's ear, which Tyson gruesomely spat onto the ground. Tyson then dodged Lane's attempt to separate the fighters and shoved Holyfield toward the corner of the ring.

After officials successfully split up the two boxers, the fight was paused for several minutes. Initially, Lane wanted to disqualify Tyson for his actions. However, he deferred the decision to the ringside physician tending to the defending champion. When Holyfield was cleared to continue boxing, the joint decision was to let the match continue. Tyson received a deduction in points for the bite.

Shockingly, Tyson tried to bite Holyfield's other ear in another clinch. This time, Holyfield's ear was left intact. Lane didn't notice the incident at first, despite Holyfield throwing his arms up in protest. The round finished uninhibited, but Holyfield brought the second bite to Lane's attention between rounds. There were visible markings from the second bite, giving credence to Holyfield's claim that Tyson bit him yet again. Seeing this, Lane halted the fight once more.

Tyson, hearing why the fight was stopped, went crazy. He launched across the ring toward Holyfield's corner, trying to attack the opposing boxer and his corner members. Security members entered the ring, surrounding the fighters and keeping Tyson away from the Holyfield corner.

The mayhem in the arena continued even as the fighters were escorted to their individual dressing rooms. It took a long 25 minutes for the final decision; Mike Tyson was disqualified for biting both of Holyfield's ears. It was the first time a fighter had been DQ'd from a title match since 1941 when Buddy Baer's manager incurred a disqualification for refusing to leave the ring in a fight against Joe Louis.

While Holyfield forgave Tyson (the two have even discussed a third fight), the Bite Fight severely damaged the reputation and legacy of Mike Tyson.

Did You Know?

- In 2022, Holyfield and Tyson teamed up to create edible, THC-infused ears as a nod to the infamous bite fight. It demonstrates the friendly relationship the two now share.

- Rapper Tupac Shakur visited Mike Tyson several times while he was serving his prison time at the Indiana Youth Center.

- When Evander Holyfield defeated Carlos De León in 1998, he became the first boxer ever to obtain the status of World Cruiserweight Champion.

- A statue of Holyfield stands outside the State Farm Arena in his home city of Atlanta.

- Tyson has had several entertainment projects after his boxing career, including a Broadway play, multiple books, podcasts, and TV shows.

- Evander Holyfield has also made many TV and movie appearances, including in *The Fresh Prince of Bel-Air*, *Nickelodeon GUTS*, *Dancing with the Stars*, *Summer of Sam*, *Necessary Roughness*, and others.

CHAPTER 4:

MANNY PACQUIAO AND FLOYD MAYWEATHER JR. IN THE FIGHT OF THE DECADE

When Manny Pacquiao and Floyd Mayweather met in the ring on May 2, 2015, it was one of the most anticipated fights in recent memory for the curators of boxing history. Both men had already led exceptional boxing careers. On the one hand, Mayweather was undefeated, boasting a 48-0 record coming into the match with Pacquiao; of his wins, 26 were via a knockout.

Pacquaio was not undefeated like his competitor but was still worthy of ample praise. His record at the time of his bout with Mayweather was 57 wins, five losses, and two draws. However, he had a higher knockout percentage in his wins (54% from Mayweather compared to 63% from Pacquiao). When Manny won, he won big.

Yet, the knockout never seemed to be the plan for these boxers. Rarely did their KOs come in early rounds. Instead, their knockout numbers were primarily a factor of exceptional boxing skill. They won by tiring opponents, countering their strategies, and exploiting weaknesses. If you do that well enough, you'll score plenty of knockouts along the way.

The boxing IQ of Pacquiao and Mayweather became a central part of the match's appeal. It wasn't just a matter of putting two of the best fighters into the ring but also two of boxing's great chess players.

Negotiations

Money has always been a critical factor in arranging boxing matches. Titles and legacies aside, fighters want to get paid, whether they win or lose. After all, they are putting their bodies on the line. If you get beaten badly enough in the ring, you may be on the mend for many months. Some boxers have to take an entire year between fights to repair their bodies and minds.

As time passes, money negotiations become increasingly more complex. Today, there are streaming services, Pay Per View numbers, international broadcasting revenue, sponsorships, merchandise, betting odds, and more. All of these factors influence how much each fighter takes home from the match. Between Manny Pacquiao and Floyd Mayweather Jr., these financial negotiations lasted years.

The first bonafide discussion of a Pacquiao-Mayweather Jr. fight was near the end of 2009. At this time, Mayweather Jr. had briefly retired from boxing. Meanwhile, Pacquiao was rocketing into the spotlight, taking down several notable opponents, like Ricky Hatton, Miguel Cotto, Oscar De Lay Hoya, Juan Manuel Márquez, and others. While Mayweather had mentioned Pacquiao in interviews, there weren't any official talks until he had a few wins under his belt after his return to boxing.

Soon enough, the two fighters were at the center of the boxing world. A fight between Pacquiao and Mayweather became all anyone wanted to see. The CEO of Mayweather Promotions stated that a Pacquaio match was the next best step from a marketing point of view. Boxing fans were also emphatic on social media about the two champions meeting.

Over the next six years, several negotiation rumors, roadblocks, and disputes would fuel the hype surrounding the fight for boxing fans. The first rumor was that Pacquiao signed a contract to fight Mayweather at the end of 2009. This turned out to be untrue. The Filipino boxer stated there were still a few things left to negotiate.

The point of contention that kept the boxers from agreeing was drug testing. Pacquiao had a known issue with blood testing too close to the fight, remarking that it made him feel weak. While he agreed to the Olympic-level drug testing requested by the Mayweather side, the testing schedule became an issue. Unable to resolve the problem, Mayweather and Pacquaio ended negotiations, and each boxer went on to fight a different opponent.

When negotiations opened for a second time (now in 2010), Pacquiao said he would agree to the outlined drug testing "as long as they're not getting a large amount of blood." Mayweather then announced he was taking a break from boxing for the remainder of the year, pausing negotiations yet again.

From 2010 to 2014, the negotiations mostly fizzled out. Pacquiao had agreed to almost any drug testing schedule, even leading up to the fight. However, the two still couldn't agree on how to split the money. Mayweather Jr. wanted to give Pacquiao a set amount for the fight without any cut of the fight's revenue from Pay Per View and other sources. Pacquiao declined, prompting Mayweather to publicly call him a "desperate dog." He went on to state the Filipino-born champion was in tax trouble.

Pacquiao was quick to reply, requesting that the two fight for charity:

> *"I challenge him to include in our fight contract that both of us will not receive anything out of this fight. We will donate all the proceeds from the fight - guaranteed prize, should there be any, gate receipts, pay-per-view, and endorsements - to charities around the world. Floyd, if you're a real man, fight me. Let's do it for the love of boxing and for the fans. Let's do it not for the sake of money. Let's make the boxing fans happy."*

Another year would pass before Mayweather and Pacquiao officially announced their fight at the MGM Grand in Las Vegas. With years of mounting hype, the fight was expected to shatter financial records, marking it as one of the richest fights ever.

Better Never Than Late

Billed as the Fight of the Century, the early rounds lived up to the hype. Pacquiao and Mayweather Jr. were both on the attack. Mayweather stood out as the more complete fighter, repelling Pacquiao's advances while countering with his own. Even when Pacquiao got him against the ropes, Mayweather escaped easily and unharmed.

Unable to score too many hits, Pacquiao lost the opening rounds. He wouldn't hit big until the 4th round. Not only did he outpunch Mayweather, but he also landed a mammoth left that sent Mayweather against the ropes. This was the theme for many of the middle rounds. Pacquiao was more aggressive and spent most of the time in the ring chasing after Mayweather.

However, Mayweather was winning rounds through his defense-first strategy. Despite the constant pressure from Pacquiao, little was getting through. It wasn't until the 7th round that "Money" Mayweather started throwing punches more freely. The offensive shift kept Pacquiao off balance for most of the later middle rounds. Whenever the Filipino champion tried to advance, Mayweather would use his jabs to keep him back and take away any momentum.

The increased aggression from Mayweather drew excitement from spectators, especially late in the 9th round when the two fighters traded a series of punches. The crowd felt they were finally seeing the fight promised. Mayweather briefly returned to a more reserved strategy in the 10th round, preferring to counter Pacquiao's punches and find strategic opportunities.

Then, in the 11th round, spectators witnessed the most aggressive Mayweather had been so far. Satisfied that this final flurry of punches was enough to win him the frame and the match, he shifted back to defense yet again. The final round was the least exciting. Mayweather did his best to avoid any contact, scarcely drawing close to Pacquiao. After the final bell, the decision was announced: Floyd Mayweather Jr. was still the undefeated fighter, winning with a unanimous decision.

Pacquiao was unhappy with the decision. He felt he was the leading fighter, never backing down from being the aggressor. The punch statistics from the fight showed a different story. Even though Pacquiao was on the attack for much of the event, Mayweather's defenses limited him to a low percentage of landed hits. Meanwhile, the defense-first boxer was more accurate with his counters and actually threw more punches in his brief but effective moments as the aggressor.

If there was one thing that Manny Pacquiao won in the fight, it was the crown for the more entertaining fighter. Many boxing fans felt the battle didn't nearly live up to the hype. It was dubbed the 'Better Never Than Late' fight because of this substantial gap between fans' expectations and reality. The long wait for the fight, combined with the expensive Pay Per View and ticket fees, made things worse. People felt they had waited years for this disappointment.

The primary reason for the disappointment was Mayweather's reserved strategy. While he was superior on a technical level, many fans slammed him for "dancing" and "hugging" instead of boxing. Even boxing legend Mike Tyson weighed in via Twitter: "We waited five years for that..."

Pacquiao still maintains that he won the fight.

Did You Know?

- Manny Pacquiao was a Senator in the Philippines between 2016 and 2022. He even ran for the presidency in his home country but was beaten by Bongbong Marcos.

- Floyd Mayweather Jr. has appeared in music videos by Ludacris, Justin Bieber, and Armani White.

- The Mayweather family is full of boxers. Floyd Sr. fought in the welterweight division and once faced Sugar Ray Leonard. One of his uncles, Roger Mayweather, won two world championships.

- Besides boxing and politics, Pacquiao has also played and coached basketball for the Terrafirma Dyip team in the Philippine Basketball Association.

- Manny Pacquiao is the only boxer in history to create his own entrance music. In fact, he has produced three albums, some of which have gone platinum in the Philippines.

- Few athletes in history have made more money than Floyd Mayweather Jr. His revenue from boxing fights, endorsements, and other deals adds up to over $1B.

CHAPTER 5:

TYSON FURY GETS OFF THE CANVAS

Tyson Fury and Deontay Wilder share one of the more respected boxing rivalries from recent years. The trilogy between the fighters is up there with some of the greatest of all time - Ali and Frazier, Pacquiao and Márquez, Bowe and Holyfield. Fury himself called it "as worthy as any trilogy in the history of the sport."

The magic of the Fury and Wilder rivalry is impossible to pin on just one component. It was part trash-talking, part controversy, part unexpected occurrences, and many parts incredible boxing by two of the best of the time.

Tyson Fury may have been destined to be a boxer since birth. His father named him after Mike Tyson, the heavyweight champion at the time. Fury was born premature, and doctors gave him only a small chance of living. The namesake was to show that Fury was a fighter and would survive.

Deontay Wilder, on the other hand, wasn't born a fighter. He was pushed into the profession by financial circumstances. Wilder had his first child, Naieya, when he was 19. Having a child at any age is a life-altering event. As a teenager, Wilder had particularly limited resources to support his new family, especially with a pile of medical bills adding up from his newborn daughter's spinal birth defect.

After a string of low-paying jobs, Wilder started rethinking his financial strategy, hoping to use his innate athleticism to his advantage. He landed on boxing as his next career path. Most people who turn to boxing for money become steppingstones for the guys with real drive, passion, and talent. Wilder was not a member of this unfortunate group. He naturally excelled at boxing - a diamond in the rough that trainer Jay Deas would shape.

Wilder's financial position worried Deas in the beginning. He had seen many people walk through the doors of his gym with similar dollar sign dreams, only to give up when the training became too hard. Wilder was another breed. "He worked just as hard when he didn't know I was watching as he did when he knew I was looking," Deas explains. "That's very unusual."

This meant that Wilder had both the exterior - athleticism, power, a tall frame - and the interior - work ethic, motivation, grit, and all the other intangible stuff - that make exceptional boxers. What he lacked was time and experience. When Wilder began competing in the Olympic trials in 2008, he only had a few years of amateur boxing experience. He often faced opponents with over twice the training time.

Fury Gets Off The Canvas

Deontay Wilder and Tyson Fury shared similar approaches to their first fight. Both fighters approached the bout with a technique-first attitude. It was not a slugfest or a wildly offensive battle. In fact, there were only a few rounds where either boxer threw more than 10 punches.

The first few rounds were particularly slow. It appeared both men were feeling the other out, trying to get a sense of one another's strategy for the fight. Aside from trading a few punches, there wasn't much to speak of until Round 4, when Wilder jabbed Fury's face enough to draw blood from the UK-born boxer's nose.

By the middle rounds, Fury shifted to a southpaw stance, hoping to pour on the punches and reclaim the fight. It seemed to work for the time. Fury backed Wilder against the ropes and kept him there, avoiding any retaliation. In the 7th and 8th rounds, the boxers traded punches, while keeping their defenses tight.

In Round 9, the crowd at the Staples Center briefly rose to their feet. Wilder knocked Fury down with a left hook and overhand right. Referee Jack Reiss began the count, but Fury was back on his feet quickly. It was less the punching power of Wilder that put him to the ground and more a loss of balance. Fury had tried to duck the left and was in a low stance when the overhand punch hit the top of his head, pushing him to the canvas.

It wouldn't be the same story in Round 12. Even though Fury had done well at outscoring his opponent in the previous two rounds, Wilder put him on his back with a devastating right-left combo. The six foot nine inches, 256-

pound behemoth hit the canvas with a thunderous boom, the kind typically only reserved for WWE matches.

Again, Reiss began to count. The count felt merely a formality to most in attendance and watching from home. No one gets back up after a hit like that, especially not from Deontay Wilder! Fury looked dazed until the referee flashed him the five-count. Then, he rolled over, rose to his feet, and stood up once again. His rise from the canvas stunned everyone. After checking Fury, Reiss permitted the fight to continue.

There weren't any fireworks left from either fighter. Fury managed to get a few blows in during the final few seconds, but that was all. The last bell rang, and the two fighters embraced in a hug, showing appreciation for the battle they had endured together.

The judges handed down their decision for the fight, declaring it a split decision draw. One judge scored in favor of Wilder, another for Fury, and the third scored an even split. However, punch stats after the fight showed that Fury landed more punches in every round except for three. Many boxing experts and fans felt Fury should have had an advantage in scoring. He was even more accurate than Wilder.

Unfinished Business

While many people in the boxing community continued to assert that the judges robbed Fury of a victory, Wilder's opinion on the draw was the opposite. "I think with the two knockdowns, I definitely won the fight." He did go on to admit that he came out slow and was hesitant in certain rounds.

While the two fighters disagreed on who was the victor, they did agree that a draw wouldn't cut it. It didn't take long for rematch talks to start. In a year, the second fight was officially announced for February 22, 2020. Fury lobbied for the fight to take place on his home turf in the UK, but it was ultimately held in Las Vegas.

Boxing fans hoping for a stellar rematch to rival the two boxers' first bout were quickly disappointed. While the second meeting of Wilder versus Fury was a memorable fight, it didn't go the distance and the fighters didn't appear as evenly matched. For one, Fury, an already sizeable opponent, was even larger than his first fight weight. He said the additional weight was intentional, hoping the added size would add power; he wanted a knockout victory.

As it turned out, Fury's plan worked. He was in control of the fight from nearly the beginning. He found Wilder many times with his jab. Defensively, Fury avoided his opponent's most substantial power swings. In Round 3, Fury crossed with a stiff right; Wilder hit the canvas only to return to his feet. The punch caused him to begin bleeding from the ear. He fell several times in the round, but they were ruled slips, not knockdowns.

The next true knockdown came in the 5th round. Fury threw a successful combination, twisting to hook Wilder in the body, who was now bleeding from both the ear and mouth. While Wilder would rise to his feet again, he didn't show much activity beyond the resilience to keep getting up. When Tyson Fury launched another successful combination in the 7th round, Wilder's corner threw in the towel.

After the fight, Wilder was quick to produce reasons for his loss. First, he threatened to fire cornerman Mark Breland for throwing in the towel. "...Do not ever throw that towel in because my pride is everything. I understand what it looks like but, when you have power like me, I am never out of a fight." Ultimately, Wilder kept Breland on his team.

Wilder also attributed the loss to an elaborate costume he wore during his ring entrance. He alleged that the heavy weight of the costume wore his legs out before the fight started. The armor-like suit weighed over 40 pounds. Then, a third reason: Wilder thought his water might have been spiked.

Fury and many other notable figures in the boxing world waved off these "excuses," which only incited Wilder further. His new claims included Fury using illegal weights in his gloves and using gypsy spell craft to weaken him. It was not the first nor last time Wilder would accuse Fury of gaining the advantage through otherworldly forces.

The Trilogy

Running out of theories about why he lost the second fight, Deontay Wilder decided to put his money where his mouth was. He activated a clause in the contract that gave the loser the power to initiate a second rematch fight. Of course, he also put his thematic spin on things. "Your king is in great spirit," he posted across social media, "we will rise like a phoenix from the ashes and regain the title. I'll see you in a few months. For the war has just begun."

The trilogy was born.

All that was needed was a place and time for the two boxers to meet. Typically, this is the easy part. The hard part is getting boxers to agree to terms, price, purse split, etc. That was all taken care of through the rematch clause. Yet, the location and date proved to be a challenge because of COVID-19.

Initially, the fight was set for July, but the pandemic pushed the date back to the fall. Then, it was pushed again to the following year. Fury's side didn't want such an iconic match to happen without fans. Since the boxer's following was primarily in the UK, this made things more complicated due to travel restrictions during the pandemic.

With so many delays, Fury tried to give up on the trilogy completely. With the dates always changing, it was hard to prepare and train accordingly. He now set his eyes on a bout with Anthony Joshua that would decide who was the undisputed heavyweight champ.

Wilder wouldn't give up, taking Fury to court for breaking the trilogy clause in their contracts. Fury countered, claiming the rematch clause had expired because of the repeated delays. Ultimately, Wilder won the claim and Fury had to end negotiations with Joshua and settle the trilogy first.

The fight was slated for July 2021, but Fury tested positive for COVID-19 in the final weeks before the fight. Once again, the fight would need to be rescheduled, and the world would continue to wait to see the outcome between Wilder and Fury.

Once and For All

On October 9, 2021, over a year and a half after their second encounter and almost three years since the first fight, Tyson Fury and Deontay Wilder finally met to end the trilogy in an event labeled "Once And For All." Despite

Fury's pleas to have at least one fight in his home country, Nevada hosted the third and final bout.

Between the unending stream of social media posts, trash-talking comments between the fighters, and the numerous delays caused by the COVID-19 pandemic, both men were eager to see this thing through. Their eagerness to quiet the other was apparent from the very beginning of the match.

At first, Wilder tipped the odds in his favor. He came out in Round 1 aggressive and in control, landing successful hard shots to Fury's body. Fury tried to re-establish himself in the next two rounds. At the conclusion of Round 3, he put Wilder to the canvas with a two-punch combination, starting with a hook to the head and finishing with an uppercut after his opponent tried to clinch.

Wilder survived the round, but the momentum of the bout had clearly shifted. Fury came out aggressive in Round 4, hoping to keep the pressure up and send Wilder to the ground again. The strategy backfired. Wilder not only avoided getting knocked down again, but he countered Fury's aggression, landing a powerful left-jab, right-cross to the head. Suddenly, it was Fury who needed to get off the canvas and survive the count. He got up only to be floored again (this time by a right hook that hit him just beyond his ear).

Once more, Fury survived the count and rose to his feet. The round was over shortly after, and the boxer got a much-needed reprieve. The next round saw yet another reversal in momentum. Now, Wilder was pouring it on, trying to knock Fury down for a third time. However, his heavy swings could not land and did little except drain his stamina. Meanwhile, Fury was able to rebound from the previous two knockdowns.

Over the next several rounds, Fury dominated, landing more shots than Wilder and even stunning him a few times with heavy punches. The more successful strikes Fury landed, the more gassed Wilder appeared. The champion appeared to be running away with the victory, a point punctuated in Round 10 when Wilder went down again from a massive right. He recovered but didn't seem to have anything left in the tank.

Fury continued to out-strike and outperform his weakened opponent for the remainder of the fight. He landed several more hits that looked to stun or hurt Wilder. Finally, a minute into the 11th round, Fury hit Wilder with a right that hit flush with the boxer's temple. He collapsed to the canvas for the third time in the fight. Referee Russell Mora wasted no time coming in and stopping the fight. Tyson Fury won the trilogy.

Hoping to end the series on a positive spot of sportsmanship, Fury went over to Wilder's corner in the post-fight chaos for a handshake. Wilder was unwilling. During an interview shortly after, Fury said, "I went over to show some love and respect and he didn't show it back. I will pray for him so that God will soften his heart… It was a great fight, worthy of the best of trilogies."

The boxing world agreed.

Did You Know?

- Tyson Fury was born in England but has Irish roots. He has represented both countries at different times throughout his career.

- After winning a bronze medal in the 2008 Olympic Games, Wilder dubbed himself "The Bronze Bomber." It was a nod to Joe Louis' famous nickname, "The Brown Bomber."

- Tyson Fury is related to several other boxers. His half-brother Tommy has been professionally boxing since 2018. Moreover, Hughie Fury, Nathan Gorman, Andy Lee, and Hosea Button are all members of the Fury family tree.

- There is a bronze statue of Deontay Wilder in his hometown of Tuscaloosa, Alabama. The bronze pays homage to the boxer's nickname of "The Bronze Bomber."

- The armor-like suit that Wilder wore in his ring entrance during the second chapter of the trilogy cost $40,000, about $1,000 a pound. It was meant to symbolize Black greatness during Black History Month.

- Fury is an outspoken advocate for mental health awareness, particularly for men. His work and stance on mental health stirred many to refer to him as "The People's Champion."

CHAPTER 6:

THE WAR FOR THREE ROUNDS

The most obvious difference between boxing and your run-of-the-mill street fight is the rules. Anything goes in a street fight, but boxing, of course, has rules, weight classes, and safety precautions. Yet, the true difference is technique. Boxing isn't about who is bigger or hits harder. Sure, these things help, but strategy and fighting intelligence are the critical aspects that matter most. It is why boxing is known as the "Sweet Science."

When an off-the-street "tough guy" enters a boxing gym for the first time, the first thing most trainers do is put him against the smallest guy available. The untrained combatant always loses, no matter the size. This isn't meant to test their mettle; it's to humble them. It's hard to maintain that tough guy attitude after being flattened by the room's tiniest boxer. It solidifies the crucial lesson that strategy trumps strength.

Boxing matches fluctuate on a spectrum between "pure" boxing and raw fighting. At times, instinct usurps strategy. A vital responsibility of a boxer's trainer and cornerman is to instruct when a fighter needs to tighten up their technique because they are deviating too much. Even with this guidance, boxers will still find themselves in slugging matches. This was the case between Thomas Hearns and Marvin Hagler when the two met in the ring on April 15, 1985, at Caesar's Palace.

Thomas "The Hitman" Hearns would change weight classes several times throughout his career, becoming the first boxer to win titles in five separate divisions (welterweight to light heavyweight). He's one of the most notable disciplines of Emanuel Steward, a legendary boxing trainer and HBO commentator, better known as "The Godfather of Detroit Boxing." Hearns swiftly gained a reputation in the boxing world for his large, slender frame that packed powerful punching power, even as he moved up weight classes.

Hearns' opponent on the April night in 1985 was Marvelous Marvin Hagler, a boxer with a reputation for an iron chin. Throughout his almost 15-year career, he was knocked down just one time. Like Hearns, Hagler also punched harder than most. He defended his title of undisputed middleweight champion across seven years and 11 fights. Ten of those defenses were knockouts.

Given the strength and toughness of both boxers, promoters accurately titled the match "The Fight." After just three rounds, it became known as "The War."

Round 1

Both men brought a sense of urgency from the beginning of the bout. There was no bad blood between the two, yet both seemed to come out of the gate seeing red. Hagler, typically a slow starter who liked to read his opponent's strategy first, charged out from the corner on the opening bell. He tagged Hearns multiple times, sending the other boxer against the ropes. The opposition found an answer quickly, responding with an epic right that smashed into Hagler's chin.

The two boxers clinched, only for a moment, before continuing to swap powerful punches. A few grueling moments later, Hearns held Hagler after receiving a hard left. The two separated once more, and the War continued. "No nonsense at all here!" Cheered the broadcasters. There was no feeling one another out or playing it smart; the two men went straight to slugging without concern.

At some point during the heavy exchanges, Hearns broke his right hand. It didn't immediately appear to hinder him as both boxers continued to swing with no regard for technique, strategy, or pacing. However, as the round clock ticked on, Hearns had to adapt to his injury. He changed his movement patterns and threw more jabs with his undamaged hand.

The steady jabs produced a cut above Hagler's eyes on his forehead. The boxer ignored the wound and continued to find opportunities to pin Hearns to the ropes and unleash punishment. Neither boxer showed any signs of slowing down or changing strategy; it was a three-minute round of pure brawling in the ring.

Not only was it honored as the best round in 1985, but Round 1 of the Hagler-Hearns bout, also tops many lists for the best round of all time. Both fighters seemed to have the same mentality - the fight cannot leave this round. They fought like the scorecard was tied in the final minutes of the match. Hearns and Hagler both appeared to pour everything into that first period. It seemed almost impossible that either would have anything left for the subsequent rounds.

The scoring for the 1st round was split, punctuating how even the two combatants were for the first three minutes. With Hearns suffering from his broken hand and Hagler wearing a stiff cut on his forehead, both men had challenges heading into the next round.

Round 2

Neither fighter could match the pace of Round 1. Hearns in particular was noticeably less active. In a future interview, Hearns admitted that he had nothing left, saying, "That first round took everything I had." Surprisingly, his primary point of fatigue wasn't his arms or broken hand; it was his legs.

"I don't like the way Tommy's moving," said Sugar Ray Leonard, one of HBO Boxing's commentators for the fight. He went on to call Hearns' movements "rubbery-legged." Hearns later confirmed the concerns of the commentators,

"My legs were gone; even before I came out, my legs felt weak." Steward, Hearns' trainer, felt the rubbery legs were a result of a massage the boxer received before the bout.

Overcoming his weakened legs, Hearns continued to find success in his repeated jabs to Hagler's face and forehead. Hagler tried to change stances, hoping to limit the impact of Hearns' jabs. When he failed to establish a rhythm with the new style, he reverted back to his southpaw approach. From his more natural stance, he found success countering the jab.

With around 30 seconds left in the round, Hagler scored a vicious combination that sent Hearns against the ropes. Then, Hagler continued to unload, landing punches to the body and head. He kept pummeling Hearns until the bell sounded to end the round.

Once again, the judges couldn't decide on a victor for the round. Two judges, Herb Santos and Harry Gibbs, still felt Hagler had a small edge, but the final scorer, Dick Young, marked the round for Hearns.

Round 3

As the third and soon-to-be final round of The War got underway, Hearns continued his strategy of relying on the jab. For almost the entirety of the round, he was backing away from the always-advancing Hagler. Hearns occasionally planted his back foot and launched a jab or two before using his long legs to skip away and give himself distance.

There was one flaw in his approach. Hearns never shook those rubber legs that Sugar Ray Leonard noticed in the 1st round. Some of his movements were awkward and off-balance. Not only did this diminish his punching power, but it also opened up opportunities for Hagler to score hits and wobble the taller boxer even more.

At around the one-minute mark of the round, Hearns repeated jabs to Hagler's face and forehead had produced a gruesome visual spectacle for fans. After clinching his opponent, Hearns threw a left hook that glanced off Hagler's face. Despite not connecting properly, it did open up the growing cut on his forehead that had rapidly worsened throughout the fight.

Referee Richard Steele noticed the blood cascading down Hagler's face and immediately paused the fight. He took the reddened boxer to a neutral corner and gave him a quick once-over. He wanted to ensure the blood coming down his face was not obscuring his eyesight, putting him in the dangerous situation of being unable to see incoming punches. The fight resumed once Steele was confident that the flow from the cut wasn't affecting Hagler's eyesight.

While he was permitted to continue the round, the opened wound put Hagler on a clock. If the bleeding worsened (and it would, with Hearns' continuous jabs), the fight would surely be stopped. Once Steele signaled for action again, Hagler jumped back to the ferocity displayed in Round 1. He continued to advance on Hearns, getting to the inside and finding his mark. Yet again, Hagler got his opponent to the ropes and orchestrated a successful volley of body blows that looked to defeat the foe.

Hearns, on the other hand, wasn't finding much success. After the brief stoppage, he landed one significant jab to Hagler's face but was largely ineffective otherwise. Rather than get a firm base to throw his jabs from, Hearns was trying to snap them off. These wilder throws weren't landing their mark as Hagler continued to march forward, blood still oozing from his forehead.

Just past the halfway mark of Round 3, Hagler slipped one of Hearns' jabs and countered with an overhand right. The swipe across Hearns' face sent the boxer stumbling and hopping to the other side of the ring. As he tried to get space from Hagler, he broke one of fighting's cardinal rules: never turn your back on your opponent.

As Hearns tried to find his footing, he turned his head and body completely away from Hagler. He even appeared to smile, perhaps to show Hagler that the blow hadn't hurt him. It didn't matter because it wasn't the punch he needed to worry about. By the time he turned to face Hagler again, it was already too late.

Hagler charged in with a right before swinging and missing with a huge left hook. Then, he leaped forward and unloaded a right cross that turned off the lights for Hearns. As soon as the tremendous hit landed, Hearns' body slumped over Hagler. Hagler stepped back to give himself space to throw more punches, but the fight was over. He landed one uppercut as Hearns' body, battered and exhausted, dropped to the canvas.

Miraculously, Hearns managed to reach his feet before the count of 10, but the boxer could barely stand. He looked like he had just left the bar after too many beers and fell into the referee's arms who immediately called the fight. The War was over, and Marvelous Marvin Hagler was the victor.

Did You Know?

- After his boxing career, Hagler turned to acting. He appeared in several action movies, including *Indio*, *Indio 2*, and *Virtual Weapon*.

- Thomas Hearns participated in a WWF match. He was challenged by Bret "Hitman" Hart for "stealing" the "hitman" nickname.

- Detroit natives may remember Hearns' other nickname, "The Motor City Cobra." The name highlighted the boxer's powerful striking power and his Detroit heritage.

- Hagler loved his nickname so much that he legally changed his name to Marvelous Marvin Hagler in 1982. He wanted the name change to encourage broadcasters and boxing networks to refer to him by the 'Marvelous' nickname.

- The only boxer to knock Marvelous Marvin Hagler down was Juan Roldán. However, the call is largely contested, with Hagler and many people in the boxing world considering it more of a slip than a true knockdown. Hagler would go on to win the fight by TKO.

- Hagler grew up in Newark, New Jersey, but his family moved after the infamous and devastating Newark riots of 1967. The Hagler family relocated to Brockton, Massachusetts.

CHAPTER 7:

A LEGENDARY FIGHT NIGHT WITH THOMAS HEARNS AND SUGAR RAY LEONARD

As time began to close the door on boxing's most significant names in heavyweight history - Muhammad Ali, Joe Frazier, Ken Norton - there was a palpable hole in the boxing world. It was the end of what many contemporaries viewed as a Golden Era for boxing, particularly the heavyweight division.

Without these bright stars, interest in boxing started to wane. America's attention shifted to a new favorite spectator sport - football. Then, four boxers rose to popularity, taking up the mantle from greats like Muhammad Ali. Marvelous Marvin Hagler, Thomas Hearns, Sugar Ray Leonard, and Roberto Duran became known as the Four Horseman, or Four Kings, of boxing.

Throughout the 1970s and 1980s, boxers from this legendary quartet would meet nine times. Every one of these bouts further solidified the four names in history and the graces of boxing fans everywhere. Some of the fights shared by members of the Four Kings are recognized as among the greatest matches of all time. This was the case when Thomas Hearns met Sugar Ray Leonard on September 16, 1981, at Caesars Palace.

The 15-round fight was titled "The Showdown" as it was the first time Hearns and Leonard met in the ring. At the time, Leonard had just one loss (against Roberto Duran, another member of the royal quartet) and 31 wins, 21 by knockout. Hearns entered the match undefeated in 32 contests, failing to KO his opponent only twice. His ability to knock out fighters established his nickname as "The Hitman." "The Showdown" was also a unification title match to decide the welterweight champion.

Hearns Gets an Early Lead

The fight began exactly as the experts expected. With titles on the line and 15 rounds to work with, neither boxer would exert too much out of the gate. Hearns consistently advanced on his opponent, using his long reach to score with the jab. With this strategy, Leonard had trouble getting close enough to retaliate. All he could do was rely on his technical boxing skills to keep himself from getting too hurt. When Hearns made minor mistakes to give Leonard opportunities to tag him, he was sure to capitalize consistently.

At the sound of the bell concluding Round 1, Leonard put his glove up to touch Hearns on the side of the head. It's unclear what his intentions were. It appeared as if it was an innocent way of acknowledging a good round. However, Hearns took it as a sign of disrespect and responded with a late punch after the bell. Leonard then mocked Hearns by wiggling his body as if to say, "You couldn't buckle me if you tried."

This altercation brought some extra intensity to Round 2. Leonard was doing a good job of avoiding most of Hearns' shots but still rarely found opportunities to get close enough. However, he did find more chances to taunt and showboat in front of Hearns, especially after deftly dodging oncoming combinations. Hearns replied in kind, smiling each time his opponent failed to tag him or he landed a hard enough punch of his own.

Taunting aside, Hearns had plenty to smile about. His strategy of using his longer reach (78 inches compared to Leonard's 74) allowed him to outscore the opposition *and* provided a defense that Leonard couldn't solve yet.

By the 4th round, Leonard was moving less. If he couldn't beat the reach of Hearns with his legs, he'd try to use his chin. He stood his ground close to Hearns, allowing him to come in and score punches but managing to return some of his own.

It was a worrisome trade-off in strategy, especially as swelling around Leonard's left eye became more and more evident. Even more troubling was that he was still falling behind in scoring. He would need even more to surge back and claim the fight.

Sugar Ray Leonard Mounts a Comeback

Sugar Ray Leonard continued to be aggressive in the early-middle rounds. After both boxers threw late swings at the end of the 4th, Round 5 witnessed Leonard maintaining closer proximity to Hearns, rather than keeping any distance. Dodging jabs and landing several overhand shots, it appeared he was starting to find a rhythm against the dominant Hearns.

In the final minute of Round 6, Leonard caught Hearns before chasing him to the corner and scoring another few hits. It was a significant turning point and the first time in the bout that Hearns appeared in trouble. The body shot forced Hearns to alter his strategy moving forward. He now had to protect his damaged ribs for the remainder of the fight.

Twenty seconds later, Hearns re-established himself and returned the favor by wobbling Leonard. The two continued to trade until the end of the round. It was the first that Leonard won unanimously, helping him make up lost ground on the scorecards.

Hearns continued to receive steady punishment from Leonard in the 7th round. Perhaps worn out from the previous six rounds, The Hitman seemed unable to match his opponent's pace. Leonard was pouring on punches, recording six- and seven-punch combos at various points in the round.

Despite being down on scoring in the early parts, Leonard now appeared destined to flatten his opponent at any moment. While Hearns managed to get his mobility back in the 8th round, he rarely advanced or used his agility and reach to his advantage as he did in the early rounds. One of the only bright spots for Hearns was that he was largely unharmed, aside from a few extended rights from Leonard. Towards the conclusion of the 8th round, he appeared to be out-boxing his aggressor, demonstrating yet another shift in momentum between the two boxers.

Hearns Takes Back Control

With seven rounds left, The Showdown was half over, and the point difference between the two boxers was razor thin. One judge had scored it a complete tie, while the other two gave Hearns a two-point edge over Leonard (75-77). After losing a series of rounds, Hearns was looking to regain control over the fight; Leonard needed to maintain his momentum during the final chapters of the bout and come ahead on points or score a knockout.

Ultimately, it was Hearns who completed his objective. He moved better than in previous rounds, no longer standing toe-to-toe with Leonard. To use the correct terminology, he was back to boxing instead of fighting. It was a smart strategy because, although he was hurting more than Leonard, he could still win on points by out-maneuvering his opponent long enough.

Hearns' strategy worked exceptionally well because Leonard had dispensed a lot of energy in the prior rounds to tip the judging scales back in his favor. Leonard's punch volume fell off in the round, meaning Hearns needed only a little offense to secure the round. At around the halfway mark of the frame, Hearns flourished some offense, finding his snappy jab again. He took the round from a relatively inactive Leonard with just a few punches. "Why has Sugar [Ray Leonard] gone to sleep?" posed the broadcast team at the end of Round 9.

With a lackluster previous round, Leonard needed to bring the action in the remaining frames. He was either unwilling or unable to negotiate roads through Hearns' defenses to strike payload. Again, spectators watched as Hearns took a round by merely dancing and bouncing around the ring, occasionally firing a jab to score points. Each time he appeared at risk of being cornered by Leonard, he'd slip away into an unoccupied area of the ring and resume his bobbing and weaving.

Hearns continued to showcase excellent boxing technique into Round 11, and his constant left-hand jabs had almost closed Leonard's eye completely from swelling. With a minute into the round, Hearns followed one of his signature jabs with a heavy right; it was possibly his best connection so far. Leonard took the punch well, but it did shift momentum in the round.

Suddenly, Hearns was on the advance while the other boxer withdrew and attempted to recover. "Look how quickly one punch can turn the dance around!" Noted one commentator. Leonard tried to use Hearns' confidence to score. He stopped drawing away and stood still near the center of the ring, attempting to coax his opponent close enough to damage his body again.

Unfortunately for Leonard's team, Hearns did a stellar job staying just far enough away to do damage without putting himself at risk. He only came in close twice; Leonard couldn't capitalize on either chance. Hearns had won another round and did exceptional damage to Leonard in the final minute.

KO Or Go Home

Sugar Ray Leonard was running out of time. There were only a few rounds left, and his eye was getting dangerously close to swelling closed completely. Hearns took advantage of this in the 12th round, throwing more from his right arm since the left side of Leonard's vision was compromised. If the abuse to his eye continued, Leonard knew the referee could call the fight off entirely if he couldn't defend himself.

In short, Leonard was in danger. He knew it; Hearns knew it; the spectators knew it. The desperation showed in his strategy. He was throwing (and missing) huge punches in attempts to put the fight away for good. Hearns looked better and better as the rounds continued. He had little trouble avoiding these power swings and countering with scoring punches.

There was no more jeering, smiling, or taunting from either of the boxers. The fanfare and mental games were over; this was all business. Leonard and Hearns even tapped one another's gloves at the end of Round 12, a sign of respect shared between a pair of kings.

In the intermission before the start of the 13th, fans in attendance were chanting "Tommy!" over and over again. Hearns got off his stool and threw his arms up to beckon the chants even louder. In Leonard's corner, the tone was not positive. Angelo Dundee, Leonard's trainer, was giving his fighter an earful. "You're blowing it now, son. You're blowing it," he started. "We need fire and you're not firing! You're blowing it. Ray, you've got to be quicker. You've gotta take it away from [Hearns]."

The motivational speech must have shaken something loose inside Leonard. He came out in the 13th round with renewed vigor. At exactly the midpoint of the round, the boxer connected with a left-right combo that staggered the always-bouncing legs of Hearns. Leonard saw the hurt and pounced.

For about 12 seconds straight, Leonard threw a flurry of everything he had. Hearns tried to protect himself by clinching, but the wild barrage from the opposition made it impossible to hold on. The unrelenting storm from Leonard sent Hearns into the ropes and then through them. It appeared to be the first knockout of the fight, but the referee ruled it a slip.

Hearns was back on his feet quickly, and the fight resumed. Leonard wasted no time resuming his fast-paced assault. There was a minute left in the round, and he intended to use every second of it to knock his opponent around the ring. For the first 30 seconds, Hearns did a good job avoiding most of the trouble, even tagging Leonard with a few punches of his own.

Then, the storm began again. Hearns barely managed to survive the round, falling into the ropes again in the final seconds. This time it was recorded as a knockdown. The boxer survived the count and the round ended. After the brief and much-needed intermission between rounds, Leonard came out in the 14th with the same intensity. He had his target back against the ropes after only seconds into the round.

Hearns fought his way free and scored a few more punches, but points weren't going to matter soon. A minute and 10 seconds into the round, Leonard connected with a massive right. Hearns staggered so much that Leonard raised his arms in triumph, expecting his opponent to hit the canvas. Instead, Hearns stabilized himself against the ropes, triggering Leonard to continue punching.

For the next 30 seconds, Leonard swung madly at his opponent. Exhausted and hurting, Hearns couldn't clinch to save himself, nor could he keep his guard up. He was on the ropes and defenseless. Referee Davey Pearl correctly stepped in to separate the boxers and award Leonard as the winner by TKO, saving Hearns from further harm.

It was yet another electric meeting between members of the Four Horseman of boxing.

Did You Know?

- Sugar Ray Leonard is the godfather of Khloé Kardashian and has appeared in several episodes of the family's hit reality TV show.

- Thomas Hearns and Sugar Ray Leonard are on a short list of only five boxers in history to win world titles in five weight divisions.

- Leonard has appeared in several movies and TV shows, often playing himself. You can see his occasional acting in *The Fighter, I Spy, LA Heat, Riot, Married with Children,* and other titles.

- Leonard won gold medals at the 1975 Pan-American Games and the 1976 Olympics as an amateur boxer.

- The Leonard-Hearns fight featured a newer 10-point scoring system (the standard used today). There was some controversy after the bout that the judges didn't use the new system correctly, awarding too many points to Hearns in rounds he lost by large margins.

- For most of his professional career, Sugar Ray Leonard worked with the same trainer as Muhammad Ali.

CHAPTER 8:

THE RETURN OF DANNY JACOBS

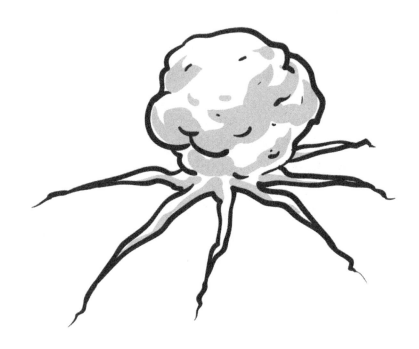

Daniel Jacobs is an active boxer as of 2023, with his most recent fight occurring in February 2022. He makes many top-10 lists for the super middleweight division, holding a professional record of 37 wins and four losses. Thirty of Jacobs' wins are by knockout, highlighting the boxer's exceptional punching power.

However, the incredible nature of Jacobs' career is not rooted in a winning record or a slew of knockouts. He is recognized because he is a fighter in every sense of the word - in the ring and outside it. His spirit and fortitude can be summed up in a single achievement: Danny Jacobs is the only boxer in history to win a title after overcoming cancer.

Changing the narrative of a career is something athletes from all sports experience. Many boxers have had to come back from injury or upsetting defeats. Jacobs' comeback was one that no one expected.

Jacobs had a promising boxing career from his very first professional fight. His first match was on the undercard of Floyd Mayweather Jr. and Ricky Hatton, a title fight for the welterweight division. It wouldn't be the last time Jacobs appeared on the undercard for a major fight, helping him build a reputation quickly.

Eventually, he'd have a chance at the WBO middleweight champion title, facing Dmitry Pirog. Both boxers were undefeated, with Jacobs the favorite to win. Things seemed to be going according to plan; Jacobs was well ahead on the scorecards. However, Pirog caught him with a right hard enough to score a knockout.

Jacobs rebounded from his first loss, but things were about to change drastically for the young boxer. In the Spring of 2011, he visited the doctor with numbness in his legs. After further testing, the doctors discovered that Jacobs had a form of bone cancer.

Osteosarcoma

Explained simply, osteosarcoma occurs as a result of a genetic cellular-level game of telephone. If you've never played the telephone game, the rules are easy. A person starts with a simple instruction or sentence. They whisper it to the next person, who re-transmits the message to the next person, and so on; until everyone has received the intel. Then, the last person performs the instruction or states the message they heard. Often, the final message is far removed from the original statement.

When cells undergo mitosis and divide, the DNA is copied and duplicated in the new cell. A cell's DNA acts as instructions, telling it what to do, just like the initial transmission in a game of telephone. In very rare occurrences, the DNA isn't transmitted properly; there's a mutation in the instructions. If too many cells receive and start following the wrong directive, problems occur.

This is how osteosarcoma occurs. Osteogenic cells - the ones responsible for forming new bone - experience DNA changes that instruct them to create new bone even though it isn't needed. The overproduction of bone creates a tumor mass. Like many cancers, osteosarcoma becomes particularly nasty when it spreads to other parts of the body.

Osteosarcoma is most prevalent in children, teenagers, and young adults because these age groups are still experiencing lots of bone growth and development, meaning osteogenic activity is high. Additionally, osteosarcoma tends to affect the legs or arms; the most common location is just below the knee. In this regard, Danny Jacobs' case of osteosarcoma was rare because of the tumor's location. While he was experiencing pain and then numbness in his legs, the actual source of the problem was osteosarcoma wrapped around his spine.

Once this discovery was made, everything became a whirlwind for Jacobs. He was rushed from the local ER to New York - Presbyterian Hospital. There, a team of surgeons, led by Dr. Roger Hartl, planned and executed a successful surgery on Jacobs' spine. Not only did they remove the cancerous sarcomaz, but they also repaired damaged sections of the spine.

Despite successful surgery, Jacobs still had a mountainous road of treatment and, hopefully, recovery. It was still not a guarantee he would survive the cancer. And the damage to his spine and the extensive surgery meant he may never walk the same way again. His boxing career was over. At least, that's what everyone believed, except for Jacobs.

Recovery

Brownsville is a neighborhood in Brooklyn, New York. It is widely considered one of the city's most dangerous areas and is frequently mentioned as the murder capital of New York City. The 73rd Precinct, responsible for policing Brownsville, is statistically the least safe area for law enforcement in New York City.

Brownsville is where Daniel Jacobs calls home. It's where he got his nickname "Golden Child," after winning so many youth boxing fights (his amateur record is an astounding 137-7). So, he had to be tough even from a young age. But nothing that the streets of Brownsville threw at him growing up would prepare Jacobs for his experiences with osteosarcoma.

Initially, his family kept the cancer a secret from Jacobs. He didn't even know he would have to undergo radiation therapy to eliminate the remaining cancer cells after doctors removed the tumor around his spine. Jacobs commends his family for holding back the seriousness of his condition.

Cancer would have been the proverbial last straw after losing a boxing career and possibly his ability to walk. He also credits his family as the primary reason for his determination to recover quickly and overcome cancer.

The second motivation was boxing. "I had a hard time growing up," Jacobs explains. "Boxing kind of served as my second family." His real motivation came when he discovered that the Barclays Center, in his hometown backyard of Brooklyn, was going to begin hosting fights. The opportunity to fight in front of his home crowd became a driving force in his recovery.

"Every day I would think about it," Jacobs remembers in an interview with *Bleacher Report*. "Through the hardest part of my therapy, and learning how to walk again, and my treatments, I always had that in the back of my mind. No matter how much it was hurting me, I just wanted to one day perform."

The hurt must have been immeasurable. Things that were once easy, not even requiring a thought to complete, were now enormous struggles. Jacobs was battling the effects of radiation treatment on top of learning to walk again.

Incredibly, only months after surgery, and against his doctors' recommendations, Jacobs went back to work in the gym. Late the following year, a cancer-free Jacobs was back in the ring. He knocked out Josh Luteran in the 1st round of his return fight. He later said, "They told me I would never box or walk again, I proved everyone wrong."

A Champion

Danny Jacobs was elated to have met his goal. He came back and performed. "The doctors resurrected me and gave me a second chance. It was a great moment in my life to be able to get back in the ring." However, his work wasn't done yet. He wasn't about to be a comeback tourist. He was a boxer.

After his victory over Luteran, Jacobs recorded two more wins before meeting Giovanni Lorenzo in the ring to settle a vacant WBC middleweight title. A year later (and another win under his belt), he returned to his hometown crowd at the Barclays Center to face Jarrod Fletcher. By knocking Fletcher out at the start of Round 5, Jacobs added to his title collection, becoming the WBA middleweight champion.

To recap, Jacobs received his diagnosis in May of 2011, including the news he may not walk normally again due to the cancer's damage to his spine. Nineteen months later, he recovers from surgery and treatment well enough to enter a professional boxing match and win. Then, in a span of less than two years, he wins five more fights, all through technical knockout or corner stoppage. Oh, and he picked up two middleweight championship titles along the way!

Jacobs would continue tacking on knockout victories. He won four title defense matches by TKO before facing Gennady Golovkin. The bout would be a unification fight, bringing together all of the middleweight titles split between the two boxers. Golovkin was a serious competitor, with an undefeated record and a history of knockout victories himself.

The match would go the full 12 rounds. Golovkin would get the victory by a unanimous decision by the judges. Despite getting the second loss of his career and losing his titles, Jacobs was the only fighter to go the distance with Golovkin. He continues to box and inspire people with his comeback story.

Did You Know?

- Growing up in Brooklyn isn't easy. Luckily, Danny Jacobs was raised by a team of powerful (and watchful) women, including his mother, Yvette Jacobs, his grandmother, Cordelia Jacobs, and his aunts. Together, they kept him out of trouble.

- Jacobs was almost a contender in the 2008 Olympic Games but lost to Shawn Estrada. Estrada went on to compete in the games, losing to the eventual gold medalist James DeGale from England.

- Early in his career, Jacobs signed with Oscar De La Hoya's Golden Boy Promotions. It was a fitting match since Jacobs' first nickname was "Golden Child."

- Shortly after his win over cancer, Daniel Jacobs started the 'Get in the Ring Foundation', helping families that have children with cancer. The foundation helps cover medical expenses, provides education on child health and nutrition, and more.

- Jacobs' godmother, Dorothea Perry, works for the New York State Athletic Commission, the body of the NY Department of State responsible for sanctioning boxing matches in the state. The two met at a boxing gym when Jacobs was a teenager.

- The surgery to remove Jacobs' tumor is typically performed by entering the patient's chest. He opted to have the surgery through his back instead, concerned his chest may not stand up to boxing punches after such a procedure.

CHAPTER 9:

BILLY MISKE FIGHTS
TO THE VERY END

Boxers take significant risks every time they step into the ring. They put their bodies and health on the line for personal glory, achievement, and the crowd's entertainment. Throughout boxing history, a handful of sad incidents have occurred where people have died in the ring or shortly after from their injuries.

These tragedies add to the mystique of boxing and hang as a perpetual warning over the door reading "Boxers Enter Here." The combatants that step into the ring are not just risking a winning record, a title, or a trophy. They put their physical well-being on the line, and sometimes their lives. Thus, boxers have to be as mentally tough as they are physically. Without this fortitude, it's impossible to thrive.

Few boxers in history have risked more stepping into the ring or exhibited greater toughness, than Billy Miske. Miske was a professional boxer active between 1913 and 1923. He likely started fighting before 1913, but there are no records of these accounts. In total, Miske participated in over 100 fights, a massive number by today's standards. His career record included 74 wins (34 by knockout), 13 losses, and 16 draws.

At a time when prizefighting was unpopular (and illegal in most states), it was easy for Miske's career to slip through the cracks. He's often underappreciated because he never held a title. That said, his boxing resume is impressive and includes wins over several famous boxers from the era, such as Battling Levinsky, Tommy Gibbons, Fred Fulton, and Harry Greb.

With only a small pool of boxers available to fight at the time, Miske would meet many of these fighters in the ring several times. For instance, after losing their first two meetings, he handed Tommy Gibbons the first draw of Gibbons' career. Miske finally found an edge over Gibbons in their fourth meeting but lost their fifth and final.

Miske had better luck against Jack Dillon. He beat the former light heavyweight champion four times in five encounters. He also split four meetings with Battling Levinsky, another champion.

His only title shot was against Jack Dempsey on September 6, 1920. It was the first time Dempsey defended his title after securing it from Jess Willard. It was also the first professional boxing match to have a radio broadcast. Although, the broadcast was delayed significantly because the station had to rely on telegraph transmissions summarizing the events of the fight instead of a live person at the ringside. Dempsey would successfully defend his title, knocking Miske out in the 3rd round.

Diagnosis

At some point in 1918, Miske visited his doctor and received a life-changing diagnosis. His kidneys were failing, and he had only years to live. He was suffering from Bright's Disease, a term that was applied to a range of different kidney issues. Miske was just 24 years old at the time and felt he had a promising career as a boxer ahead of him. This diagnosis changed everything.

Bright's disease gets its name from Richard Bright, who first began studying various symptoms and their correlation to kidney problems in 1827. The disease became a catch-all diagnosis for a wide range of kidney-related issues. As research became more sophisticated, the term fell out of use with the discovery of more specific kidney diseases.

Thus, it's unclear what exactly was wrong with Miske's kidneys. No matter the specifics of the issue, the reality was certain - Miske's life was coming to an abrupt end. Initially, he was only given months to live. Boxing was out of the question. If Miske was hit in his failing kidney, he could die in the ring. With no cure available at the time, his only option was to rest and relax as much as possible until the disease took his life.

Most people would have listened to the doctor's recommendations, but Miske had a problem. He had accrued a substantial debt, reportedly in excess of $100,000 (almost $2M by today's standards). Miske had invested in a car distributorship that wasn't doing well. Unfortunately for Miske, cars were still seen as a luxury. Henry Ford had not yet invented the famous Model T that would help make owning an automobile more affordable.

Determined to avoid leaving his family in a mountain of debt, Miske continued to box, knowing that any fight, or any day, could be his last. In fact, the St. Paul native would cram as many fights into his last dying days as he could, totaling over 30 fights after receiving his diagnosis of Bright's disease. When he challenged Jack Dempsey for the title, it was over a year after he received the news of his illness.

Each fight became harder and harder, but Miske continued. Eventually, he became so ill that even training was too taxing. Somehow, he still appeared in the ring against legendary opponents. His decline makes his lifetime record even more impressive as many of his losses came at the end of his career and life. Even more awe-inspiring, is that he *won* many fights, despite his body's severely weakened state.

Miske kept the diagnosis a secret from almost everyone, including his family. He worried that, if anyone knew, they would prevent him from boxing anymore. As time passed and his deteriorating shape became more evident, he brushed off his wife's questioning by saying he had some kidney trouble, but it was nothing serious. He didn't want her to worry.

One Last Fight

Billy Miske's manager, Jack Reddy, had also become concerned by the fighter's weakened state. He was possibly the only person Miske fully confided in about his condition. It wasn't that Miske trusted his manager more than his family. He likely would have never told Reddy either if he didn't have to.

Reddy was the one responsible for arranging matches for Miske. The sicker the boxer got; the more unwilling Reddy was to put him in the ring. When the time came for Miske's last fight, he hadn't fought in over a year. The boxer spent most of his time in bed, too weak to get up. He hardly even resembled a boxer anymore.

Miske's plan was to compete in one final fight, taking whatever money he earned to give his family the best Christmas of their lives. At first, Reddy was unwilling to be Miske's accomplice. His concerns were understandable; Miske looked as bad as he probably felt. The manager didn't want to be responsible for what may happen if he put his client into the ring in his current state.

Reddy pleaded with Miske to at least start training. After all, he looked as thin as a matchstick. Miske stated this wasn't possible. "How could I put you in the ring like this?" Reddy may have asked the boxer. Miske didn't care. He was dying anyways. He could die on the couch or in the ring, what did it matter? Ultimately, the manager caved and went off to arrange a fight.

For his last professional boxing match, Miske would fight Bill Brennan. This was not an easy opponent. Brennan had already gone the distance in 12 rounds against Jack Dempsey. The one positive to choosing him as Miske's final opponent was Brennan's most recent fight. On March 12, 1923, Brennan fought Luis Angel Firpo. It was a lopsided match, and Brennan was hospitalized for a week after.

Brennan's team anticipated his retirement after the tremendous loss to Firpo. The injuries he sustained were nothing to sneeze at. Of course, Miske's condition was much worse. Perhaps, Brennan took the fight hoping to end with one final win. It's unclear if he had seen Miske or knew about his weakened state.

Again, Miske was in bad shape and too sick even to train. It's reported that the first time he even put gloves on was the moment he stepped into the ring versus Brennan. Luckily, Brennan also appeared to have neglected much of his preparations for the fight. Still recovering from the injuries, he arrived looking out of shape.

With two fighters in far-from-perfect conditions, it's easy to expect that the Miske-Brennan match would be a lackluster fight. Remarkably, the deteriorating Miske came out swinging. For months, he'd scarcely left his bed, but here he was, landing punches against Brennan. In the 3rd round, he hit Brennan hard enough to stun him. A round later, Miske landed a knockout blow on his opponent. He didn't just survive the fight; he won it.

For his victory against Brennan, Billy Miske walked away with $2,400. With Christmas only a month and a half away, he knew exactly what to do with his winnings.

Christmas Morning, 1923

Christmas is the source material for many beloved stories and films. *Miracle on 34th Street, Die Hard, It's a Wonderful Life, A Christmas Carol, How the Grinch Stole Christmas* - none of these stories is possible without the Christmas season. Yet, there is one Christmas story in the Miske family that is loved more than all the others.

Early on Christmas morning, Billy Miske's three children, Donna, Billy Jr., and Douglas, raced downstairs, as kids do on this most special of mornings. What they saw in the living room of their Minneapolis home was a scene unfathomable by their young minds. There were presents everywhere!

This is 1923; there are no Hollywood films depicting extravagant Christmas mornings or giant feasts. All the Miske children know is what they've seen with their own eyes, and they had never seen something like this.

There was a baby grand piano for Donna. A brand-new train set for Douglas and Billy Jr. Even the couch and the chair in the living room were new! It would have been impossible to find a happier trio of children in all of Minneapolis that Christmas morning. The only one more thrilled may have been Miske himself, admiring the joy of his children and his wife. For months, he had lived off boiled fish. Now, he sat before a grand feast with his family.

Just six days later, on January 1, 1924, Miske's kidneys could no longer keep fighting. He died having had a successful boxing career for many years - more than most can claim at age 30. Despite his shortened career, he is still remembered as one of the top boxers of all time.

Most importantly, Miske left this earth having given his family the Christmas morning he knew they deserved. He should be a role model for families and fathers everywhere. He took up an immense burden to spare his family from hardship.

Did You Know?

- Miske's kidney issues were enough to keep him from serving in World War I. However, the boxer did his part by contributing to Red Cross benefits.

- Billy Miske Jr. followed in his father's footsteps, participating in several professional boxing matches in the late 1930s. His career record includes 16 wins (almost all by KO) and 10 losses.

- Many of Miske's presents to the family on his last Christmas became heirlooms treasured across generations.

- Miske's boxing nickname was 'The Saint Paul Thunderbolt' because of his speed and punching power.

- All three of Miske's children are now deceased, but the story of their father's sacrifice continues to inspire new generations in the family. Several of Miske's grandchildren have tattoos of boxing gloves adorned with thunderbolts in his honor.

- Jack Dempsey and Billy Miske were good friends outside the ring. When Dempsey knocked Miske down in their famed fight (the only recorded time Miske was knocked down in his career), he helped the Minnesota native up and to his corner.

CHAPTER 10:

WRONGFULLY INCARCERATED DEWEY BOZELLA GETS HIS FIRST FIGHT

Dewey Bozella ended his boxing career with a 1-0 record, which doesn't sound like much of a fighter to mention in a book about incredible boxing stories. What makes Bozella's 1-0 lifetime record so compelling is the unfortunate road he had to take to reach his professional boxing debut.

No road to the ring is complete without a few bumps. For Bozella, his path was an uphill battle from the very beginning. At age nine, Bozella's father killed his pregnant mother and fled, abandoning the young boy and his siblings.

The fate of the Bozella family continued to be a sad one. One of his brothers died in a stabbing, a second was shot to death, and a third died from AIDS. With few opportunities or the security of a family behind him, Bozella turned to crime. He would spend close to three years in prison for attempted robbery.

After his release, Bozella found himself in trouble again. He was charged with the 1977 murder of Emma Crasper from years earlier. The police alleged that Ms. Crasper caught Bozella in the middle of a burglary, and he killed her before fleeing. Despite his pleas of innocence (and a lack of evidence for a crime from several years ago), he was sentenced to 20 years to life.

Bozella spent 26 years in prison for a crime he didn't commit. It took almost three decades for him to prove his innocence, clear his name, and regain his freedom. Shortly after release, Bozella, now 52 years old, began his path to his first professional boxing match.

Prison

Dewey Bozella had been arrested shortly after Emma Crasper's murder. However, he was let go due to a lack of evidence linking him to the crime. The case was reopened six years later after two inmates claimed Bozella was responsible. They traded the "information" for their early release.

The inmates' testimony proved to be enough evidence to convict Bozella, even though he wasn't a match for a fingerprint left on the scene. That print matched an individual responsible for similar crimes in the area, but the prosecution never followed up on the lead. They were fixated on framing Bozella.

After his conviction, Bozella was sent to Sing Sing Correctional Facility in Ossining, New York (formerly Ossining Correctional Facility). This maximum-security facility has a reputation for housing some of New York's most dangerous criminals.

Aside from the prison's occupants adding to its reputation, the facility's history also paints a grim picture of life inside its walls. For years, inmates were not allowed to make any unnecessary noise, including talking to one another. The marble stone from which the prison is built also added to the eerily quiet atmosphere. This practice didn't last and was abolished long before Bozella's arrival.

Sing Sing was also home to New York's Death House. This was a specific section of the prison built to house and ultimately execute people on death row. A total of 614 inmates (men and women) were executed in this section of the prison by electrocution. The most high-profile executions at Sing Sing were - Julius and Ethel Rosenberg, a couple convicted of conspiracy to commit espionage. They were found guilty of sending top-secret information to Soviet Russia in 1951.

Despite the dangerous company around Bozella at Sing Sing, he was a model prisoner in every respect. He spent much of his time bettering himself and pursuing avenues to have his wrongful conviction overturned. He earned a bachelor's degree from Mercy College and then a master's from the New York Theological Seminary. He would have undoubtedly been granted parole if the board didn't demand that he admit guilt.

One of the few bright spots of his time at Sing Sing (second only to meeting his wife, of course) was boxing. Bozella became the light heavyweight champion in Sing Sing, boxing for 10 years while incarcerated. The remainder of his time was spent training other fighters before the prison's boxing program was shut down.

Considering Sing Sing was home to some of the most dangerous criminals in the state, Bozella's boxing opponents in prison were serious competitors. He even fought against Lou Del Valle. Valle, the future light heavyweight champion, was 19 at the time, but still a Golden Gloves champ when the two fought. "I thought I had him," remembers Bozella. "I had him stumbling. But I got careless, and he hit me with a three-punch combination."

During his time in Sing Sing, Bozella maintained his innocence. He was even refused parole several times because he wouldn't admit guilt, despite being a model prisoner. The case even went to trial a second time in 1990, but the verdict remained unchanged. Eventually, Bozella sought help from the Innocence Project.

Wrongful Conviction Overturned

With the assistance of lawyers from WilmerHale, the Innocence Project reopened Bozella's case again. Typically, the Innocence Project looked at DNA evidence. This sophisticated and accurate analysis method didn't exist when many wrongful convictions happened. Prosecutors often relied on eyewitness accounts, footprints, fingerprints, etc. This makes Bozella's conviction all the more troubling since the evidence available, a fingerprint, was largely ignored in favor of testimony from unreliable sources.

In Bozella's case, no physical evidence remained to analyze. It had been destroyed at some point during the boxer's incarceration. Instead, the WilmerHale team had to take a different approach. They uncovered evidence that was never presented to Bozella's original defense. Not only did this prove his innocence, but it also showed the unscrupulous measures the prosecution used to incarcerate the man wrongfully.

When the case reached Supreme Court Justice James Rooney, he agreed with the WilmerHale team. Bozella was innocent, and the key evidence proving this had been withheld during the original trial. On October 28, 2009, Bozella was finally released from Sing Sing as a free man.

After Bozella's release, the lawyers at WilmerHale continued to fight for him. They pursued a lawsuit against Dutchess County, NY, pushing for restitution for the years Bozella spent in prison. The legal team discovered that the key evidence omitted from the original trial was withheld by the Dutchess County District Attorney of the time. Several police officers were also connected with framing Bozella.

Thanks to this overwhelming evidence against the county, Bozella received a settlement of $7.5M.

Freedom to Fight

Upon obtaining his freedom, Dewey Bozella continued his passion for boxing. He worked at boxing gyms to train teenagers and teach them about the dangers of criminal life. His goal was to open his own gym for troubled teens. He also became a public speaker, sharing the lessons his experiences taught him.

ESPN became interested in Bozella's story in 2011. At the ESPY Award Show, they highlighted his life and awarded him the Arthur Ashe Courage Award. It was an incredible honor; he joined a small group of recipients that includes names like Muhammad Ali and Nelson Mandela.

While attending the ESPYs and receiving his award, Bozella stated it was his dream to have one professional boxing match and experience the thrill of being in a real boxing ring. After all, had he not been wrongfully sent to prison, he may very well have had a successful boxing career.

Bernard Hopkins, a light heavyweight champion at the time, heard Bozella's dream and decided to step in and make it a reality. Bozella's story had struck a familiar chord with Hopkins, who had grown up under similar circumstances. He was from a rough neighborhood in Philadelphia and turned to crime at a young age. He even served several years in prison for a slew of crimes. Upon release, Hopkins turned to boxing as a means to escape the criminal life.

Hopkins was scheduled to fight Chad Dawson on October 15, 2011, just a few months after the ESPY Award Show. He arranged for Bozella to participate on the undercard and face Larry Hopkins (no relation). He also set Bozella up with a boxing trainer to get him ready. Of course, Bozella didn't need much preparation; he'd been ready for this fight his entire life.

Bozella's fight against Larry Hopkins started slow. Bozella, 52 at the time, tried to feel his opponent out, who was looking for his first professional win. By Round 2, he began to flash the boxing talents that had earned him the title of the light heavyweight champion of Sing Sing Correctional Facility. It didn't matter that his opponent was younger; Bozella had experience. At the end of four rounds, he was declared the winner by unanimous decision.

After, he retired from his professional boxing career, stating it was a young man's game. Yet, he had finished what he set out to do. He stepped into a professional boxing ring, as a free man, and won.

Did You Know?

- The Sing Sing Correctional Facility is named after the Wappinger Native American words "sinck sinck." This translates to "stone upon stone." It refers to the marble stone construction of the prison.

- Bozella published a book in 2016 titled *'Stand Tall: Fighting For My Life, Inside and Outside the Ring'*. The memoir details his life experiences and time in Sing Sing.

- After his one and only professional fight, Bozella became a trainer for young boxers, providing a role model to keep troubled teens out of gangs and away from criminal activity.

- Bozella is far from the only boxer to serve time in prison. Sonny Liston, Mike Tyson, Edwin Valero, Diego Corrales, Dwight Muhammad Qawi, and many others have done time.

- There is now a Sing Sing Prison Museum near the correctional facility that details the history of the building.

- The Innocence Project website cites 243 wins for wrongfully convicted clients as of 2023. This includes almost 200 exonerations by DNA evidence alone. In the process, the Innocence Project has identified 84 people actually responsible for the crimes.

CHAPTER 11:

A WORLD AFFAIR: JOE LOUIS VERSUS MAX SCHMELING

In 1936, the world watched tentatively as Nazi Germany, under the Fuhrer Adolph Hitler, underwent significant militarization. Hitler ignored conditions outlined in the Treaty of Versailles that prohibited Germany from maintaining a military presence in certain territories.

While the United States and Nazi Germany wouldn't officially be at war for another five years, tensions between the two nations were very high. Newspaper headlines from the time accurately paint the picture of the American people's views with regard to Nazi Germany.

The *Philadelphia Evening Bulletin* on March 7, 1936, had headlines like "Washington Sees France Defied," and "Hitler's Actions a Direct Challenge to Paris." The stories went on to say, "Will guns boom again on the Western Front? This question absorbed the Capital today, as officials tensely watched Adolf Hitler's remilitarization of the German Rhineland."

Before US and German soldiers exchanged artillery on the battlefield, two men - American Joe Louis and Max Schmeling of Germany - took to the ring for a fight that would mean so much more in a world on the brink of war.

The First Fight

German, American, and world audiences tuned in to hear the outcome of the Schmeling-Louis fight via radio broadcasts. Around 57 million people listened on June 19, 1936, with 45,000 lucky enough to see history in the ring at Yankee Stadium in New York City.

By size, the two boxers were practically doppelgangers. They weighed within a couple of pounds of each other, with Louis at approximately 197 pounds and Schmeling at 194. In height, the men were less than an inch apart. Both fighters shared a reach of 76 inches. The biggest difference between the two was their preparation prior to the fight.

The overall expectation was that Joe Louis would beat Schmeling without any trouble. Listening to this popular belief, the Brown Bomber didn't put much effort into his pre-fight preparation. He was enjoying women, food, golf (a new passion), and life in Hollywood.

Meanwhile, Max Schmeling was studying Joe Louis with a near-fanatical dedication. He watched films on Louis again and again, even playing them in reverse to find hidden hitches in his target's stance and boxing approach. His studying helped him find the patterns and tells that would allow him to anticipate Louis' every move.

One thing Schmeling detected was a chink in Louis' defenses. When the Bronze Bomber threw more than one left in a row, he dropped his guard between punches. This meant that, for a fraction of a second, Louis was completely vulnerable to a right, which happened to be Schmeling's best punch.

This discovery enabled him to devise a strategy to counter the fighter's usual approach. All he needed was to get Louis to throw punches (easy), watch for a left, and look for the slight lapse in defense. Then, he could unload with his stiff right. He was so confident in his plan for the fight that he publicly stated he had a winning strategy against Louis. Most, including Louis and his team, felt the boast was purely to build up a buzz for the fight.

Unfortunately for Louis, it wasn't just a boast; Schmeling had found a serious gap in the American's style that he would exploit for 12 rounds. Schmeling threw left jabs casually, baiting Louis to get close and throw with his left hand. Once the German spotted that ephemeral moment where his opponent didn't have his guard up, he'd twist his body to launch a devastating right cross.

Through the first rounds of the fight, Louis was at a clear disadvantage. He couldn't seem to penetrate Schmeling's defenses and was taking repeated jabs and those artillery-like crosses. Louis' complete ineffectiveness was a shock to fans. Worse yet, his eye was swelling and appeared cut. It would soon be impossible to score the knockout punch he needed to win.

The fight ended in the 12th round. Schmeling landed a two-punch combination - a right to the body followed by a second right to the jaw - that put Louis to the floor. Referee

Arthur Donovan counted to 10, and Louis didn't get to his feet. It was the first knockout of Joe Louis' career.

Schmeling would later admit about the first fight that the two were made for each other: "Louis's one weakness matched perfectly with my greatest strength, the one which I had made my career."

Schmeling and Nazi Germany

The fight was over, but its impact would still be felt for months to come. Joe Louis had become a hero to Black Americans. Taking on Schmeling was an opportunity to extend his reach as an icon to all Americans by defeating Germany's prized fighter. By losing the fight, he became the target of significant criticism. Even African American-owned newspapers lambasted him for the loss to Schmeling.

Adolf Hitler was quick to turn Schmeling's win over Louis into propaganda supporting the strength of Nazi Germany. Joseph Goebbels, Hitler's head of propaganda, used Schmeling's likeness to show Germany's superiority over the US. While proud of his German heritage, Schmeling was not a supporter of the Nazi Party. Yet, he became a valuable propaganda tool for the Nazi Party.

After the fight, the German press quoted Schmeling:

> *"At this moment I have to tell Germany, I have to report to the Fuehrer in particular, that the thoughts of*

all my countrymen were with me in this fight; that the Fuehrer and his faithful people were thinking of me. This thought gave me the strength to succeed in this fight. It gave me the courage and endurance to win this victory for Germany's colors."

It's unclear if these were Schmeling's actual sentiments or remarks manufactured by the Nazi propaganda machine. Goebbels inserted many fabricated quotes from Schmeling over the years, many mentioning the superior race, which the boxer never believed in. "I am a fighter, not a politician. I am no Superman in any way."

Schmeling's indifference to Hitler's politics turned to disdain the more his name and likeness was used to push Nazi ideals. When Hitler offered him the Dagger of Honor, he refused. The Fuehrer was not exactly the type of man you wanted to embarrass or turn down. Schmeling also stayed with his manager Joe Jacobs, who was Jewish.

In response to his defiance and non-affiliation with the Nazi Party, Schmeling was kept under tight watch. He couldn't go anywhere without his publicist, a crony of Goebbels. This ensured he wouldn't speak out against the Fuehrer or his politics. His wife and mother were also prohibited from traveling with him, nullifying the threat that he might defect.

Sadly, the use of Schmeling's name in the German press and Nazi propaganda made him a very unfavorable person in America.

Rematch

The second fight between Schmeling and Louis was a complete turn-around from the first bout. Schmeling took to the fight with the same strategy that won him their first meeting. He kept himself straight up and planned to use his left to jab at Louis and set up the cross.

What was Louis' plan? An all-out assault. He wanted to beat Schmeling and beat him badly. The strategy was simple: throw everything you have in the first three rounds. By Louis' estimation, the fight would be over in the 1st or 2nd round. He even told sportswriter Jimmy Cannon to expect a first-round knockout.

Louis let Schmeling come in close, dodging and feinting a pair of punches. Then, he unleashed an unrelenting barrage of his own. The fight was briefly stopped halfway through the 1st round. Louis was swinging so consistently and accurately that referee Arthur Donovan needed a moment to check Schmeling. When the fight resumed, Louis went right back to work. He promptly knocked his opponent down with a right hook.

Schmeling rose only to be sent back to the canvas again. Louis hit him with a series of three punches to the jaw. Once more, Schmeling hit the ground and popped back up, needing only two seconds the count to get to his feet. However, he was hurting from Louis' constant pressure.

Logic suggests that Louis would be the one gassed and out of energy. He had been throwing punches since practically the moment the first bell rang. Yet, it was Schmeling who didn't seem to have anything left. Louis couldn't be tired. He was carrying his race and his country on his shoulders.

Out of stamina, Schmeling struggled to keep his hands up to defend himself. Now, Louis could batter his German foe with almost no regard for his own protection. He put Schmeling back on the ground for a third time after another repeated barrage of punches flush to the head.

With 54 seconds still left in the round, Max Machon, Schmeling's cornerman, entered the ring to stop the fight. He didn't need to. Donovan had already called it, deeming Schmeling unfit to continue the bout.

Punch stats from the round clearly show how lopsided the match was. Louis threw 41 punches in total, landing around 75% of them. Conversely, Schmeling managed to throw just two punches at the very start of the round.

The outcome of the Frazier-Schmeling rematch helped bolster American patriotism. Louis' victory was a major win for the country but particularly for African-American advancement. It was one of the true successes for Blacks in that era.

In Germany, Hitler's propaganda machine gave up on their star boxer, a silver lining for Schmeling. However, as World War II began, Hitler would require Schmeling to participate as a paratrooper. Luckily, his military service was short-lived. Eventually, stories of his defiance of Hitler and the Third Reich would reach American ears, changing perceptions of the boxer and painting him as a hero.

Did You Know?

- Max Schmeling holds an odd record as the longest-lived heavyweight champion. He died at the age of 99 in 2005.

- Schmeling is the only boxer in history to win a world heavyweight champion title on a foul.

- No boxer has ever defended his title so completely as Joe Louis. He won 25 consecutive title defenses, holding the honor for 12 years. Both are records across every weight class.

- The movie *Rocky IV,* which pits the character Rocky Balboa against Ivan Drago, is loosely based on the Schmeling and Louis fights, updated to fit world tensions surrounding the Cold War.

- Schmeling and Louis became great friends later in life. When Louis fell into financial hardships, Schmeling provided assistance. He even covered part of Louis' funeral costs and was a pallbearer for his friend and famed opponent.

- In 1962, Louis participated in the San Diego Open. It is considered one of the first times an African American was allowed to play golf during a PGA Tour event.

CHAPTER 12:

THE SLUGFEST TRILOGY BETWEEN MICKEY WARD AND ARTURO GATTI

Mickey Ward and Arturo Gatti are not boxers that typically find themselves high on people's lists for the greatest of all time. Yet, the two are remembered for sharing one of the best trilogies in boxing's history, including one match that makes many lists as one of the greatest *fights* ever.

Both had reputations for being tough and durable boxers, which made their fights incredible spectacles for fans. It was a matter of two immovable objects clashing in the ring. "I used to wonder what would happen if I fought my twin. Now I know," Gatti remarked after their second encounter.

The boxers were so closely matched that, no matter who won or lost, both fighters needed medical care after. Two of the three matches were named 'Fight of the Year' by *Ring Magazine,* and the 9th round of their first match was named one of the best of the century by Emanuel Standard, a legendary boxer in his own right and a commentator for HBO Boxing.

Gatti and Ward also had histories of unexpected comebacks in matches. As a younger fighter, Gatti knocked down Wilson Rodriguez after repeatedly enduring punishing barrages from the opponent. Ward stunned every boxing fan and his opponent, Alfonso Sanchez, when he dropped him with a body shot in the 7th round after scarcely landing a punch since the start.

Ward's upset was arguably one of the most shocking of all time. The broadcast team heavily criticized him throughout the fight. The collective sense was the fight may be stopped because Ward wasn't throwing enough punches. Referee Mitch Halpern even told him he needed to show something, or he'd stop the fight.

"Someone should pay *me* to watch this," commented Roy Jones Jr, remarking on how disappointing the match was. On cue, as if he heard the comments himself, Ward delivered two body blows to Sanchez. The second one, a kidney punch, ended the fight. "Is that a lucky punch or did Mickey Ward just make idiots of us all with a spectacular piece of strategy?"

With their proficiency in come-from-behind and unexpected victories, any fight between these two boxers could dramatically shift at any moment. Boxing fans anticipated the kind of edge-of-your-seat viewing that normally is only reserved for title matches between the biggest names in boxing. Gatti and Ward's trilogy did not disappoint.

Arturo Gatti Versus Mickey Ward I

The fight between Gatti and Ward had all the trappings of a title fight without the title. With Ward hailing from Lowell, Massachusetts, and Gatti growing up in New

Jersey, it made perfect sense to promoters to host the fight at Mohegan Sun Casino in Uncasville, Connecticut. Fans of both fighters could easily commute to watch the match.

Gatti's typical fighting style was as a brawler. Yet, the early rounds saw a more calculated and technical boxer. On the scorecards, this strategy was working, granting him wins in the early round. He had also opened a wound around his opponent's right eye. Ward, on the other hand, wasn't showing much action beyond watching Gatti and defending himself.

Ward began changing his passive strategy in the 3rd round, throwing and landing more punches. While the punches didn't seem to damage Gatti, they did begin to lower his defenses. It appeared as though he was shifting back to his more natural style as a brawler. This opened him up to a handful of clean body shots by Ward.

Between rounds, Gatti's trainer, Buddy McGirt tried to get his boxer to stick to the game plan. He was worried Gatti would open his defenses too much if he resorted to a more aggressive approach. McGirt's concerns became realities in the next round. Ward absorbed a few punches before landing a heavy right to Gatti's head. Gatti started throwing more combinations, opening himself up even more. Ward took the opportunity to work his adversary on the body and head.

Gatti dispensed some of his hard punches, including a hard center body shot that put Ward to the ground. The punch landed just below the belt, which Ward punctuated by slamming the canvas in frustration. Referee Frank Cappuccino deducted a point from Gatti for the illegal low shot. The round would end as Ward was recovering from the punch.

By the conclusion of the 4th round, the physical trauma both men had endured was visibly apparent. In addition to the bleeding around his eye, Ward was now leaking from his nose. In the other corner, Gatti's right eye was swelling.

The 5th round saw Gatti in full brawler mode. He swooped in with heavy combinations, plus clean hits together against Ward, before dropping back to prepare for the next assault. Ward, meanwhile, seemed unphased. He was eating shots that would have dropped most fighters and continued to advance after each combination. Better yet, he was sending plenty of his own in return.

The spirited exchanges only grew more intense as the seconds fell off the clock. Each fighter seemed determined to tip the round in their favor. Gatti would pound shots across Ward's body and head. Then, Ward would return the favor. Gatti again. Ward.

In the final 30 seconds, Ward slammed Gatti with a combination of head punches that sent the man into the ropes. Recognizing Gatti was hurting, the Massachusetts native kept swinging. He threw punishing uppercuts to the head and hooks to the body until the bell rang. Gatti looked battered, and his swollen right eye had begun to bleed. He looked like a man barely able to stand. Ward returned to his corner, looking over his shoulder in disbelief that his opponent hadn't dropped.

Gatti's corner again emphasized that the fighter needed to stay defensive and stick to a technical strategy. While he was landing successful blows, he was taking too much punishment in return. Gatti needed to stay on the move if he wanted to outlast Ward and take the decision. He listened, and the next few rounds saw a more cautious boxer in Gatti. He managed to stave off most of Ward's attacks.

Unfortunately for Gatti, it seemed he had already taken too many punches. By the end of Round 8, he appeared out of stamina. After more shots to his body, Gatti's movement slowed considerably. Ward began to repeat his act from Round 5. He scored powerful punches to Gatti's head and body and sent him stumbling into the ropes yet again. Once again, Ward seemed determined to end the fight, and again Gatti outlasted the round time.

It was already one of the greatest fights in recent memory and deemed an instant classic. No one watching or in attendance could have anticipated that the fireworks were far from over.

Round 9

The 9th round of this initial fight between Gatti and Ward appears on many lists for the greatest ever. Sometimes, it's at the very top of the rankings. It seemed impossible, given how much each fighter had endured and exhibited thus far, that either had the energy to keep going.

Initially, Ward went straight back to work. He knew Gatti was gassed and likely wouldn't be able to evade him for the length of another round. The assessment was accurate, to a point. Gatti was certainly hurting and didn't have the feet to keep moving. It appeared more like he was leaning into punches than avoiding them. Each time Gatti tried to create distance, Ward closed it instantly.

After only a few seconds in the 9th round, Ward landed a pair of left hooks from the head to the body. The crowd at the Mohegan Sun Arena erupted, thinking this had to be the end. Even the broadcasters thought Gatti was done. "It's not like a head punch," remarked one commentator, hinting at the heavy shots Gatti had taken to the body.

To everyone's surprise, Gatti rose before the final second of the count. Although, he was visibly in pain. When the round resumed, Ward pressed even harder. Since Gatti was too hurt to protect himself sufficiently, Ward had free range to throw his punches uncontested. Punch after punch, Gatti continued to stand. More accurately, he continued to be sent staggering around the ring, from rope to rope, as Ward worked him.

Ward used Gatti like a training dummy for almost half a minute until he no longer had the energy to keep punching. No one, especially Ward, could believe that Gatti was still on his feet. This was a boxer that only a minute earlier barely got to his feet from a body blow. Even more incredible was that Gatti was now advancing on Ward! He had allowed Ward to punch himself to exhaustion - and now there was an opening to return fire.

There was little technique or strategy left in either man. Gatti was throwing his entire weight into his punches, landing often. The mammoth blows pushed the target every which way. It was the comeback no one expected from the man everyone couldn't believe was still standing. Gatti even managed to get Ward against the ropes, keeping his target still enough to keep delivering payback.

Gatti had already demonstrated his willpower to keep going; now it was Ward's turn. Astonishingly, he too had incredible strength to keep going after taking hard punches. Each time Gatti landed a successful combination, Ward appeared to nod or gesture for more as if to say, "Is that all you've got for me, Arturo Gatti?"

It felt like the two fighters had agreed to end the fight in Round 9, no matter what. They traded blows back and forth.

Once one boxer would punch himself into exhaustion, the other would pick up the mantle as the aggressor.

Ward initiated a heavy offensive towards the close of the round. *Again,* Gatti's head and body bounced around under the unrelenting blows of the attacking Ward. It appeared like the fight was about to be over. Spectators had already lost count of how often this thought crossed their minds. Each time, Gatti and Ward persisted.

When the round ended, the broadcast revealed the impressive punch stats for each boxer. Gatti landed 69% of his punches (42 out of 61) in Round 9, while Ward connected 73% of the time (60 out of 81). These numbers show what an offense-forward point this was in the match.

Round 10 was not nearly as notable. Gatti regained enough of his composure to go back to technical boxing. He kept Ward at bay and let the final minutes of the 10-round match run out. The slugfest was over.

A Trilogy Is Born

The judges returned a victory for Ward, but only by a narrow margin. No matter the outcome, both fighters had shown legendary grit in the ring. There was little-to-no hesitation from either fighter to sign up for a rematch. In just six months, the two were back in the ring together.

In the second meeting, Gatti would get the best of Ward. Even though both men got plenty of licks in, Ward was staggered badly in Round 3, colliding head-first into the corner. Once he got up, Gatti came in swinging again, landing punch after punch. Ward managed to retaliate at the end of the round but had taken a substantial beating.

The rest of the rounds followed a similar pattern. Gatti landed more punches, but not without taking some from Ward. By the mid-rounds, Gatti looked in worse shape, especially with a swollen left eye. Yet, it was clear that he was ahead on scoring, finding plenty of opportunities to work Ward's body.

By the time the rematch reached Round 10, both fighters had punched themselves out of energy. At times, they were leaning against one another, still throwing punches and putting on a show spectators expected after their first fight.

The judges' unanimous decision for Gatti was a welcomed outcome for boxing fans. It meant that a third fight between these two was inevitable. That third and final fight was another back-and-forth firework display. Gatti got ahead of Ward on the scorecard, but Ward came back in Round 6, flooring Gatti at the close of the round.

Once again, both fighters poured everything into the ring throughout the whole fight. Rarely was there a dull moment; it was nonstop, punch-trading action. When the judges announced their decision, Arturo Gatti was declared the winner by unanimous decision and the victor of one of boxing's most thrilling rivalries.

Did You Know?

- Mickey Ward is on a small list of boxers to earn *Ring Magazine's* 'Fight of the Year' honors for three consecutive years. The others are Rocky Marciano and Carmen Basilio.

- Much of Mickey Ward's boxing career and comeback story is captured in the 2010 film *The Fighter*. Mark Wahlberg was nominated for best actor at the Golden Globes for his portrayal of Mickey Ward.

- Arturo Gatti was born in Cassino, Italy, and grew up there before moving to Montreal, Canada, and then, as a teenager, New Jersey.

- Ward took a multi-year break from boxing, earning a living, by paving roads in his hometown. He saved enough for surgery on his right hand, an issue he cited for his departure from boxing. The surgery helped him return to his preferred career path.

- Gatti is in the International Boxing Hall of Fame, retiring with 40 wins (31 by KO) and just nine losses.

- The passing of Arturo Gatti made headlines when authorities believed it was a homicide. Deeper investigations concluded Gatti took his own life, but the results were disputed for many years because of the mysterious circumstances surrounding his death.

CHAPTER 13:

THE RUMBLE IN THE JUNGLE

ZAIRE

Muhammad Ali is boxing's greatest fighter in both skill and notoriety. He's what Babe Ruth is to baseball, or what Michael Jordan is to basketball - names that are known well beyond their respective sports. He's largely considered the greatest boxer of all time, captivating audiences with his exceptional style in the ring during the 60s and 70s.

Before he obtained his status as boxing's "Great One," he had to face another iconic name in the history of the ring - George Foreman.

Considering Ali's immense legacy today, it's hard to imagine him as an underdog in a fight. But, against Foreman, that's exactly what he was. The odds were 4-1 in favor of the then-undefeated Foreman. Overcoming the odds, Ali managed an upset and handed Foreman his first loss by implementing clever strategies to tip the scales.

The Road to the Rumble in the Jungle

An integral part of Muhammad Ali's legacy was what he did outside the ring and his views on civil rights. Shortly after defeating Sonny Liston and taking the title of heavyweight champion, Muhammad Ali changed his name from Cassius Clay to the one he is better known by today.

Ali no longer wanted to be called by what he began referring to as a slave name. He was never a slave himself, growing up almost a century after slavery ended in 1865.

145

Nor was his father, who he was named after. However, the namesake came from Cassius Marcellus Clay, a former slave owner turned abolitionist. "He may have gotten rid of his slaves, but held on to white supremacy," Ali stated. His new name honored his conversion to Islam.

It was just one example of Ali's commitment to civil rights advocacy.

When the United States engaged in war with Vietnam, Ali spoke out once again. He considered himself a conscientious objector because of his religious views, stating, "War is against the teachings of the Qur'an. We are not supposed to take part in wars unless declared by Allah or The Messenger."

He had other reasons for his refusal to participate in the conflict in Vietnam, stating, "I ain't got no quarrel with them, Viet Cong. Why should they ask me to put on a uniform... and drop bombs and bullets on brown people in Vietnam while so-called Negro people in Louisville are treated like dogs and denied simple human rights?"

His defiance against Selected Service laws landed him in hot water. It was a crime that carried five years in prison and hefty fines. Despite the risk, Ali held to his views against the war. Luckily for the boxer, he never served any actual time in prison. He was granted a bond while his case was under appeal. However, he lost his boxing license and titles for his controversial views on the war.

It would take three years of appeals for the case to reach the Supreme Court and Ali's conviction to be overturned. During Ali's hiatus from boxing, George Foreman made a lot of noise in the boxing world. After winning the gold medal for heavyweight boxing in the 1968 Olympics, Foreman made quick work of the professional heavyweight division.

He had overwhelming victories against key opponents. He defeated Joe Frazier in a fight dubbed "The Sunshine Showdown." Both boxers were undefeated, but Frazier was the title holder and favored to win. Foreman changed perceptions when he repeatedly knocked Frazier down six times in two rounds. While Frazier still got to his feet, referee Arthur Mercante called the fight. Foreman went on to beat Ken Norton in two rounds also. Norton and Frazier were the only two to have beaten the great Muhammad Ali at the time.

The undefeated Foreman seemed unstoppable, but he had yet to test his mettle against Ali. With Ali's conviction overturned and his boxing license restored, the two could finally meet in the ring.

Zaire

Don King was the wizard behind arranging the match between Ali and Foreman. Nervous that another promoter might swoop in, King offered a considerable purse to the boxers of $5M. At the time, King didn't have access to this kind of money. He also lacked the funds and connections to arrange the fight in the United States. So, he looked outside the country for a possible venue, ultimately landing on Zaire (present-day Democratic Republic of Congo).

An advisor of Mobutu Sese Seko, Zaire's president, urged the leader to host the fight. He agreed, hoping the spectacle would draw attention and tourism to the country, so he could continue to lead the people of Zaire unchecked.

With the event site secured, King now had to organize funds. He went through his Rolodex and called anyone and everyone he could think of to invest. The financial backing ended up coming from several sources, including Risnelia Investment, Hemdale Film Corporation, and Muammar Gaddafi, the de facto leader of Libya.

Interestingly, the two boxers had very different receptions in Zaire. In a cultural blunder, George Foreman arrived with his two German Shepherds by his side. He was unaware that it was the same breed of dogs the Belgians had used to intimidate the people of Zaire during the country's colonization. Zaire had secured its independence only 12 years before the fight.

Ali connected more easily with the people of Zaire and quickly became their favorite. His rebuking of Selective Service laws in the US and his history as a civil rights activist aligned with the contemporary attitudes of post-colonial Africa.

The interest in and adoration for Ali as a cultural, political, and sports icon was a continent-wide sensation. The people of Zaire (and those that had flocked to the country to behold The Greatest) followed him everywhere, revering him as a hero of the people.

When Ali went for his daily run, a massive crowd followed him, chanting "Ali boma ye!" repeatedly. That translates to "Ali, kill him!" Foreman's time acclimatizing to and training in Zaire could not have been easy with the city of Kinshasa chanting for his demise!

Ali's underdog status by the oddsmakers only furthered the local population's love for him. He may not have been the overall favorite, but the home crowd was overwhelmingly on his side.

The Rumble

The Rumble in the Jungle, as the fight was named, was originally set for September 25. After Foreman received a bad cut on his eye from a sparring accident, it was pushed to October 30.

In the 1st round, Ali defied expectations and his own typical fighting style. Rather than approaching Foreman with his famed speed and technical style, Ali took an aggressive charge. If the intent was solely to throw Foreman off, it appeared to work. The local favorite was able to land several right-hand lead punches. Once the initial surprise subsided, Foreman began landing punches of his own.

In the 2nd round, Ali displayed a strategy that would become synonymous with his name. Instead of advancing on Foreman like in the last round, Ali allowed himself to get backed against the ropes. He remained there, shelling up and turning his body in ways that deflected Foreman's punches. Ali wasn't hurt by any devastating blows because he kept his head out of reach. Foreman exerted immense energy throwing punch after punch but barely scored points for any clean hits.

When Foreman would stop to catch his breath or plan his next combination, Ali would throw jabs to the face. They weren't particularly hard punches; that wasn't the point. The objective was to keep Foreman frustrated so he would keep throwing punches and over-exert himself.

Whenever the two fighters clinched, Ali added to Foreman's frustration with verbal jabs. Ali was known as the "Louisville Lip" for his penchant for and proficiency at trash-talking opponents. Taunting Foreman enraged the undefeated champion, just as the opposition planned. "They told me you could punch, George!" Ali would say. He also leaned on Foreman during clinches, making the other fighter hold his weight up, thereby sapping even more of his stamina.

Foreman recounts hitting Ali hard in the jaw - hard enough for a knockout. "I thought he was just one more knockout victim until about the 7th round. I hit him hard to the jaw and he held me and whispered in my ear, 'That all you got, George?' I realized that this ain't what I thought it was."

By the mid-to-late rounds, Foreman was out of energy. His famed punching power was nonexistent, as was his ability to defend himself completely. Ali took advantage, staggering him with swift combinations. In the 8th round, Ali produced a five-punch combination that knocked Foreman to the ring floor. The undefeated champ rose to one knee, but the fight was already over.

Muhammad Ali was back in the saddle as the world's heavyweight champion, putting to rest any thoughts that his brief exile from boxing had made him rusty.

Did You Know?

- Foreman became even more of a household name later in life when his name appeared on a line of fat-reducing, portable grills. The George Foreman Grill became a sensation, selling millions of units and netting Foreman far more than he ever earned in the ring.

- Foreman returned home from the 1968 Olympics with the gold medal for the heavyweight division.

- Legendary martial artist Bruce Lee studied Muhammad Ali's exceptional footwork and body movement, incorporating them into his Jeet Kune Do fighting style.

- Muhammad Ali appeared in a DC comic book titled *Superman vs. Muhammad Ali*, depicting the superhero and famous boxer squaring off against one another.

- Ali has a star on the Hollywood Walk of Fame. It is the only one mounted vertically, instead of on the ground. Ali requested this because he shares the name of the Islamic prophet. He didn't want people to walk on the name.

- Will Smith nearly won an Oscar for his portrayal of Ali in a film of that name. Smith initially turned down the role, but Ali reached out and requested he accepts the honor. Ali joked with Smith saying, "You're almost pretty enough to play me."

CHAPTER 14:

THE RIGHT FROM ROCKY MARCIANO

The 1940s was an uncertain time for the entire world. World War II raged on in Europe, Africa, and the Pacific. Americans of all walks of life and professions would be called to war, including boxers. This created gaps of inactivity in many boxers' careers, either from serving firsthand or being unable to find opponents because so many fighters were overseas.

"Jersey" Joe Walcott was one of the many boxers with a career impacted by World War II. On February 12, 1940, just 67 days after the Japanese bombed Pearl Harbor and prompted the United States to enter the war, Walcott lost to Abe Simon. His next fight wouldn't be until June of 1944, over four years later.

With the war over and boxing back in full swing, Walcott wasted little time. From the fight in June 1944 to the end of 1947, roughly a three-and-a-half-year period, he participated in a whopping 22 fights, averaging a fight roughly every two months and winning most of the bouts. His final fight in 1947, against the legendary Joe Louis, was Walcott's first shot at the title. He lost by a razor-thin margin in a split decision.

Less than a year later, Walcott and Louis rematched, but the outcome was only worse for Jersey Joe; he lost by knockout in the 11th round. Still without a title, Walcott moved on from Louis, facing Ezzard Charles to claim a vacant NBA heavyweight title. Again, the New Jersey native was unsuccessful.

Fast-forward to 1951, and Walcott and Charles are at it again in a title match. By now, Walcott was 37 years old, a fossil in the boxing world, but he was determined to claim a title. When Charles successfully defended his title again, Walcott asked for another rematch with the stipulation that, if he won, Charles would get a chance at *another* fight to reclaim his title.

In July 1951, Walcott finally experienced the unique thrill of winning a championship title. He bested Charles by means of a knockout in the 7th round. A year later, he allowed Charles to take the honor back. Then, Walcott won again by a unanimous decision from the judges.

His next opponent had been on the warpath in the heavyweight division, stacking 42 straight wins, the majority by knockout. His name was Rocky Marciano, the "Brockton Blockbuster."

The Complete Package

In baseball, scouts use the term "five-tool player" to describe someone that has every desired quality. A five-tool player can hit, hit for power, field, run, and throw. Rocco Francis Marchegiano (he would change his name to Rocky Marciano after an announcer couldn't pronounce his last name) may be the closest representation of a five-tool boxer in history.

He had tremendous punching power, evidenced by his 87.8% knockout-to-win ratio - the highest of any heavyweight boxer. Marciano also had nonstop energy, throwing punches relentlessly, even into late rounds. That same incredible stamina helped Marciano stay mobile, and be an ever-moving target for his opponents.

When he did get hit, the Massachusetts-born boxer had an iron chin. He was only knocked down twice in his entire career, which spanned 49 professional matches. The second time was in the last fight of his career. Marciano's durability enabled him to keep moving forward on opponents, presenting himself as a constant offensive threat. It became tiresome for other boxers to keep him away. It also meant he could eat punches and throw counters of his own.

The most important tool in Marciano's indomitable arsenal was his boxing IQ. Sure, he had absolutely devastating punching power and the durability to take punches himself, but no one maintains an undefeated record over 49 fights without using their head. It was his intelligence in the ring that helped him find opportunities to unleash those earth-shattering punches that dropped so many of his opponents to the canvas.

The Old Versus the New

Opinions on who would win the fight between Marciano and Jersey Joe were mixed in the boxing community. While many fans and experts felt the younger (and also undefeated) Marciano would have the edge due to his age alone, there was another adamant school of thought that felt Walcott's experience would shine. Walcott, of course, agreed with the latter. He planned to show this young and cocky kid from Brockton how a real boxer fought. "If I don't lick him, take my name out of the record books," Walcott declared, adding that Marciano "can't fight."

The beginning of the fight seemed to showcase what Walcott and his supporters believed: experience trumps youth. The older boxer allowed the less-experienced Marciano to over-extend himself, leaving him vulnerable to a potent left hook. The power punch plastered Marciano on the canvas. It was the first time in the boxer's professional career that he was knocked down.

Marciano got back to his feet quickly, before the count even hit five, and the fight resumed. The younger boxer continued to eat heavy punches from Walcott, who seemed determined to prove to everyone that he wasn't the old, tired boxer that Marciano fans suggested.

Things continued this way through the next couple of rounds. It wasn't until Round 4 that Marciano really started to find the mark with his punches. He used his strength and durability to stick to Walcott's inside. With Marciano feeling a rhythm in his offense, the fight's intensity picked up significantly. Both boxers threw colossal punches at one another. Each time one landed, it was an astonishing feat that the recipient remained on his feet.

The shining moment in these early rounds for Marciano was when he managed to get Walcott against the ropes. He got a few clean shots against his older opponent before receiving a healthy dose of replies. The frenzied pace of the bout was as thrilling as it was terrifying. It seemed like both fighters could knock the other out at any given moment.

Throughout all these wild exchanges, Walcott was still getting the better of Marciano on points. Despite being older than his competitor, Walcott was the elusive one. He dodged many huge, sweeping swings from Marciano, countering with his own. The younger boxer seemed more willing to use his chin to take the leather of Walcott's gloves than rely on his legs to avoid the punches.

As the fight extended into the later rounds, Walcott continued to expand his gap over Marciano. Worse for the younger boxer, his inability to slip punches was catching up to him. He was having trouble seeing out of one of his eyes, making it even harder to protect against the vicious barrages from Jersey Joe. Once Walcott understood his opponent's visibility was diminished, it was open season.

Between the swelling around his eye and various cuts across his face, Marciano was losing on both fronts. He was behind on scoring and had more visible damage. Each time Walcott landed another shot, it conjured more blood from Marciano, presenting a risk that the fight may be stopped if his injuries became too severe.

For 12 complete rounds, Jersey Joe Walcott had dominated Marciano and shattered any thoughts that he was too old, slow, or any other adjective, to face a younger opponent. His superior skill and technique shined brightly through the entire fight. Coming out for Round 13, Marciano, his face swollen and hurting, too far behind on points, had one shot to maintain an undefeated record and take the title: a knockout.

Marciano, running out of rounds and time to put an end to Walcott, advanced on his opponent in Round 13. His opponent kept his distance, backing himself up and trying to land shots on the stalking Marciano. Then, Walcott felt the ropes against his back. He threw a punch to back Marciano off, but the young challenger also snapped a shot off.

Like gunslingers in a showdown at high noon, both men drew their weapons - vicious right hooks - then cocked and fired at the same time. Marciano's bullet of a punch hit first. His gloved fist landed flush on Walcott's jaw. It is considered one of the hardest and most decisive punches ever landed; it was the type of punch from which no one, not even a champion, comes back.

Jersey Joe Walcott folded, held up only by the ropes. Marciano threw one final punch as referee Charlie Daggert came in to stop the fight. It wasn't necessary; Walcott was already out.

The rematch between the two boxers was not nearly as eventful. Although, it did have a similar outcome. Both fighters appeared to stick to the same strategies from the first fight. After all, Walcott was well ahead on points; he just needed to avoid another knockout.

Marciano, perhaps accepting that he couldn't out-box Walcott, jumped straight to throwing power punches. It didn't take long for one to land. After just 35 seconds, Marciano adeptly made Walcott miss with one of his jabs. Then, he countered with a two-punch combo that started with a sharp left hook and ended with an uppercut. Walcott got back to his feet but not in time for the count. He would retire after the rematch, defeated.

Marciano continued defending his title, holding the championship honor until he retired, still undefeated, in 1956.

Did You Know?

- Some movie buffs incorrectly suggest that the Sylvester Stallone movie franchise *Rocky* is named after Rocky Marciano. The movies are actually based on a little-known boxer named Chuck Wepner. The name "Rocky" is merely coincidental.

- Joe Walcott played a role in *The Harder They Fall*, a film about a fictional boxer thrust to the pinnacle of prizefighting through a series of fixed matches. The film is remembered as the last time the famous Humphrey Bogart appeared on the silver screen.

- During his amateur boxing career, Marciano, along with some friends, participated in tryouts for the Fayetteville Cubs, a North Carolina baseball farm team for the Chicago Cubs. The boxer was cut after three weeks.

- Later in life, Walcott served as the county sheriff of Camden, New Jersey, the first African-American to hold the position. He was also a chairman of the state's athletic commission.

- Bronze statutes of Marciano exist in his hometown of Brockton, Massachusetts, at Brockton High School, and in Ripa Teatina, Italy, where Marciano's father, Pierino Marchegiano, was born.

- Walcott was the referee during the second match between Muhammad Ali and Sonny Liston. After the controversial ending of the match, which many blamed on poor refereeing, Walcott was not asked to be a third man in the ring again.

CHAPTER 15:

THE FIGHT FOR THE GREATEST OF ALL TIME

Rivalries in sports make for some of the greatest stories. The 2004 Boston Red Sox snapping an 86-year World Series drought wouldn't have been as magical if they didn't come back from 0-3 against their rivals, the New York Yankees first.

The 1950 Snow Bowl is a legendary college football moment *because* it featured two bitter rivals, Ohio State and Michigan State. It's not a Miracle on Ice if Team USA plays the Netherlands or Norway. It had to be Russia!

Boxing has many rivalries in its long history, but none as great as Muhammad Ali and Joe Frazier. It is commonly considered one of the best rivalries in all sports. The two men began as friends but quickly turned to bitter enemies when conversations about who was the greatest of all time arose.

Their trilogy was a unique treat to boxing and sports fans. It was the rare occurrence where two of the best to ever enter a ring hit the peaks of their careers at the same time. Imagine if Lebron James and Michael Jordan had played against each other!

Boxing fans were doubly lucky because the two didn't just clash in the ring once, but *three times*. The first and third fights are considered some of the greatest in boxing's history. Every bit of the Frazier-Ali rivalry lived up to the hype and more.

Fight of the Century

Muhammad Ali held the title of heavyweight champion until 1967. The honors were stripped from him (along with his boxing license) after he refused to participate in the Selective Service System during the Vietnam War. While Ali was removed from boxing, Joe Frazier dominated the scene, beating every opponent in his way until claiming the vacated titles.

The moment Ali's boxing license was reinstated, the wheels began turning on a Frazier-Ali meeting. Billed as "The Fight of the Century," it would be the first and only time that two boxers, both undefeated and both champions, met in the ring. Frazier would be defending the title that Ali had lost due to his political beliefs. The fight would settle who was the unequivocal greatest.

The hype surrounding the fight was inescapable. It became the story that the public could not, and did not, want to ignore. Every newspaper, talk show, and family dinner included a heavy dose of Ali-Frazier fight talk, from coast-to-coast, city to countryside, bar room to the boardroom.

The fight had underlying themes that cut into some of the hot-button issues facing the country at the time. Ali had become a symbol of the anti-establishment counterculture prevalent in the US. Conversely, Frazier supported the government's involvement in Vietnam, representing the other side. It became more than just a boxing match to many people.

By the time the bout started, millions of people were tuning in to watch history take place. They didn't yet know that the "Fight of the Century" would live up to its name. It was the type of fight you'd expect from the two greats. Ali got the edge early, staying at a distance and using his superior reach to bop Frazier's face as often as he could.

However, all this activity and his perpetual dancing around the ring took a toll on Ali's stamina. He couldn't keep the same pace by the middle rounds, enabling Frazier to assert himself. The boxer had built a reputation behind his deadly left hand. He was about to show Ali just how lethal that left hand was.

In the middle and late rounds, Frazier caught Ali with his left several times. Referee Arthur Mercante would later say that both fighters threw some of the best punches he'd seen - high praise from someone that had been in the ring hundreds of times with top-tier boxers. The most damaging of these punches came at the very beginning of Round 11. The punch was enough to drop Ali to his knees. However, it was never recorded as an official knockdown.

For the remainder of the round, Frazier battered Ali, sending him from corner to corner with heavy punches. The stripped champion seemed out on his legs for long stretches, relying on the ropes to keep himself standing. T he shift in momentum from Ali to Frazier was enough to give Smokin' Joe an edge on the scorecards. When the final bell rang after Round 15, the judges handed down their decision. Joe Frazier had handed Muhammad Ali his first loss and retained his title of heavyweight champion.

Ali would spend the months after the fight publicly criticizing the judging and officiating. He also sought a rematch with Frazier. In the second meeting between the two, there was far less on the line. Frazier had lost his championship status to George Foreman a year prior, receiving the first loss of his career by a tremendous Round 2 knockout. Meanwhile, Ali split a pair of fights with Ken Norton, losing the first and claiming the second.

The rematch went the full 12 rounds. Ali changed his offensive strategy from the first fight and had a slight edge over Frazier in scoring. Defensively, he held Frazier repeatedly, taking away his power on the inside and from his left hand.

This tactic sparked controversy and outrage from Frazier's team. While it is legal in boxing to clinch and hold your opponent, Ali would hold Frazier behind his neck, which is not permitted.

Legality aside, the strategy worked, and Ali won his first fight in the soon-to-be trilogy with Frazier. This would become a sticking point when the Ali and Frazier camps met to negotiate a third and final fight.

Strategic Negotiations

After the success of the "Rumble in the Jungle" bout between Muhammad Ali and George Foreman, other small international countries saw the appeal of playing host to major boxing events. Ferdinand Marcos, president of the Philippines, was quick to sponsor the event, hoping it would bring attention (and money) to his country.

When the fight's location was announced, Muhammad Ali, always the trash-talking antagonist, said, "It will be a killa and a thrilla and a chilla when I get the Gorilla (Frazier) in Manilla." And thus, the fight became known as the "Thrilla in Manilla." Ali continued to sing this rhyme whenever he was interviewed about the fight. It was a mental strategy, one that he hoped would get his opponent mad. "I like to get a man mad," he told sportswriter Dick Schaap. "When a man's mad, he wants you so bad he can't think. So, I like to get a man mad."

The negotiations for the fight brought up the controversial holds from the earlier fights. Eddie Futch, Frazier's cornerman, strategically blocked Zach Clayton from refereeing the match. Clayton was the third man in the Ali-Foreman fight and didn't call any illegal holds on Ali (of which Futch alleged there were plenty.) Instead, he encouraged the Filipino officials involved in the arrangements to use one of their countrymen to referee. They agreed and put Carlos Padilla Jr. into the ring.

169

Muhammad Ali's camp had their own victories in the pre-fight negotiations. They successfully lobbied for a larger ring, giving their boxer more room for his famous bobbing, weaving, and dancing. Ali also set the glove size to eight ounces, a lighter and less padded variety than the standard for heavyweight matches.

Again, this played into Ali's strategy for the fight. He knew Frazier was a slow starter, meaning he'd have time in the early rounds to use the light, unpadded gloves to potentially land a knockout hit or hurt Frazier enough to hamper his activity in later rounds.

The fight was set to take place at the Araneta Coliseum on October 1, 1975, at 10:00 am. local time. The arena was one of the largest of its kind and had more than enough capacity for the native and international boxing fans ready to watch two of the greats finish the trilogy. However, the time of the fight would quickly become problematic.

The early time helped correct the difference in the time zone for US audiences. There is a 12-hour difference between the Philippines and New York City. This meant that the fight at 10:00 am. local time aired live during primetime hours between 7:00 and 10:00 PM, depending on which side of the country viewers were watching.

However, the sun was nearly at its zenith by the fight's start, meaning the aluminum roof of the enclosed arena was baking in the sun, as was everyone inside the coliseum. It was akin to getting into a hot, sunbaked car with the doors shut, air off, and windows up. Add the heat from the ringside lights and the thousands of spectators packed in tightly, and you've got a recipe for heat stroke. Frazier estimated the ring temperature to be above 120 degrees Fahrenheit. Ali said he lost five pounds during the fight from sweat and dehydration.

The temperature inside the coliseum didn't slow Ali's trash-talking. As the two met in the middle to hear the rules and instructions from the referee, he verbally poked Frazier. "You don't have it, Joe!" He shouted over the referee. "I'm going to put you away." The opposition seemed unfazed. Frazier simply smiled and said, "We'll see."

The Thrilla in Manilla was underway.

The Thrilla In Manilla

The beginning of the fight went according to plan for Muhammad Ali. As Frazier stood near the center of the ring, Ali circled him and kept him back with a steady helping of left jabs. At times, Ali would blend the jab into successful combinations, staggering Frazier a few times in the early part of the bout. Frazier couldn't find a way to get inside on Ali. When he occasionally trapped Ali in a corner, Frazier's opponent would clinch and back him up to escape.

Aggravating matters for Frazier, he had to endure constant taunts from Ali. "Come on, you ugly Gorilla! Hit me!" Ali would shout as he circled and popped Frazier's face with jabs. Ali would also wave his hands to gesture Frazier forward, taunting him as if to say, "I dare you to try to get in close!"

By Round 3, Ali had dispensed a lot of energy. To help recover, he deployed his famous rope-a-dope tactic, leaning on the ropes for support to regain stamina and letting Frazier punch himself till he was tired. Typically, Ali would slip out of the ropes once his opponent was vulnerable and then reply with a savage volley of his own.

Unfortunately, Frazier was a better fighter than Ali gave him credit for. The rope-a-dope strategy also gave Frazier the crucial opportunity to get inside on Ali, which he'd been hungry for since the beginning of the fight. He was able to land several clean shots to Ali's body.

Seemingly unhurt by the blows, Ali continued to wave Frazier on, drawing laughter and cheers from the audience. At the very end of the round, Ali came off the ropes and threw some punches of his own, if only to put himself in contention for winning the round.

Round 5 was a pivotal point in the match and a huge win for Frazier's team. For one thing, the boxer's rhythm and timing seemed to improve, meaning he was slipping punches and landing more of his own. The telling point was when Frazier, known for dominating with his left and not his right, caught Ali with a right hard enough for him to take notice.

It meant that Ali had to be wary of *both* sides from Frazier. And, reinforcing his protection from the right could expose himself to Frazier's left, the more deadly of the two punches.

Later, Angelo Dundee, Ali's trainer, would state that the rope-a-dope was the wrong play because it opened the door for Frazier to pressure Ali's body and cause him to drop his guard. The strategy that had given Muhammad Ali a victory against Foreman was becoming his greatest detriment against Frazier. Whenever his back landed against the ropes, Frazier landed, too.

As early as the 6th round, Frazier started finding substantial gaps in Ali's defenses and landing hard shots with his powerful left hand. Many of the punches were enough to drop most fighters, yet Ali persevered, drawing gasps of disbelief from spectators. The punches humbled Ali. According to those ringside, Ali entered the next round shouting to his opponent, "They told me Joe Frazier was washed up." "They lied," replied Frazier.

For the rest of the fight, there was no showboating or taunting - no more mind games. It was just Frazier and Ali at center stage boxing. Both men were hot, weary, and hurting. The only strategy at play was to hit and not get hit.

Through all the exchanges, Frazier's face was swelling greatly, making it difficult for him to see punches coming from Ali's right. Meanwhile, Ali came into his corner between rounds and reported it was the closest he had ever been to dying.

Ali and Frazier continued the abuse for several more rounds. Each one faced moments that seemed to spell the end. Yet, the two boxers continued to prevail. However, the longer the event went on, the more the scales tipped in Ali's favor. Frazier's eyesight decreased each round. In the 13th and 14th frames, Ali snapped Frazier with several hard blows. Now, it was Smokin' Joe that shocked spectators by staying on his feet.

Round 14 came to an end, and both men went into their corners. While Ali was landing more punches, he was visibly out of it. Between the heat and everything that had happened in the ring, there just wasn't anything left. Later, Ali would say of the fight that he was close to giving up, even telling his corner to cut his gloves off because he had nothing left. He explained, "Frazier quit just before I did."

Frazier tried to protest his corner's decision to throw in the towel, but Eddie Futch had seen enough and delivered the final word to the referee. It may have the right call at just the wrong time. Ali was visibly spent.

When word reached his corner, he had to hold the ropes to stand and raise his hand in triumph. He only took a few steps away from the corner before appearing to fall to the ground, requiring a stool for several minutes. As he gave his victory speech, his corner helped him to his feet. Ali couldn't stand on his own and fell onto the stool again.

The Thrilla in Manilla, the trilogy, was over. Muhammad Ali fought down to the very last drop of energy and won. Ali had the final word about him and Frazier, "He is the greatest fighter of all times, next to me."

Did You Know?

- Joe Frazier has been cartoon-ized by *The Simpsons* twice, first in 1992 in the episode "Brother, Can You Spare Two Dimes?" and again in 2006 for "Homer's Paternity Coot."

- Frazier has authored two books. The first was an autobiography about his life and time in the ring. The second book, *Box Like the Pros,* is a compendium of boxing information - history, techniques, training regimens, a list of top boxing gyms, etc.

- During the first fight between Frazier and Ali, an FBI office was burglarized, exposing several documents related to the Bureau's COINTELPRO operation. COINTELPRO was an illegal FBI surveillance effort targeting American citizens. Muhammad Ali was one of its targets.

- When HBO broadcasted the "Thrilla in Manilla" match to audiences, it was the first time a television network used satellites to send the signal. This innovation changed the world of television programming.

- The Ali Mall in the Philippines is named after the legendary boxer. The multi-level shopping center, the first of its kind in the Philippines, is close to the Araneta Coliseum where the "Thrilla in Manilla" fight occurred.

- Toward the end of his boxing career, Frazier took to music, putting together a soul and funk fusion group named "Joe Frazier and the Knockouts." They recorded their last single in 1976 and even toured Europe, though attendance at their concerts was small.

CONCLUSION

There's no escaping the dangerous, brutal nature of boxing. It is the closest we'll ever come to the gladiators in the Roman Colosseum battling to death.

The people that choose boxing as their profession possess qualities not found in your average humans. They have the courage and strength to step into the roped battlefield to pursue a dream, no matter the consequences.

Outside the battleground, spectators and fans observe not merely for entertainment but also for the privilege of witnessing something transcendent, even sacred. It is the singular experience where human resolve is tested in such a dramatic and lucid fashion.

It is the chance to observe intangible human qualities - determination, courage, pain, sacrifice - in superb clarity.

The greatest boxing stories, like the 15 discussed in this book, offer the sharpest images of these immaterial components central to human identity.

They are examples that showcase the biggest triumphs of boxing's greatest warriors. At times, these stories explain the wider reach of boxing, including its impact on culture and history, which truly reflects its power.

Printed in Great Britain
by Amazon

40671802R00106